GREAT CAKES

COUNTRY LIVING

GREAT CAKES

Home-Baked Creations from the *Country Living* Kitchen

From the Editors of *Country Living*

HEARST BOOKS
A division of Sterling Publishing Co., Inc.

New York / London
www.sterlingpublishing.com

Contents

Foreword   7

Introduction   9

Baking Basics   13

Recipes

    German Chocolate Cake   22
    Carrot Pistachio Cake and Cupcakes   25
    Grandma's Applesauce Cake   26
    Berry-Dotted Angel Food Cake   29
    Pear Upside-Down Cake   30
    Blueberry Hill Cheesecake   33
    Easy Chocolate Party Cake   34
    "Hot" Chocolate Cake   36
    Chocolate Peanut Cheesecake   38
    Big-Top Carnival Cake   41
    Fresh Fig Cake   43
    Gingerbread Stack Cake   45
    Peppermint Cake   46
    Spice Pound Cake   49
    The Kitchen's Hummingbird Cake   50
    Banana-Caramel Cake   53
    Skillet Cake with Carmelized Pears   55
    Fresh Strawberry Cake   56
    Burnt-Sugar Pound Cake   59
    Toasted Coconut Coffee Cake   60
    Red Velvet Cake   62
    The Kitchen's Chambord Layer Cake   65
    Rich Chocolate Layer Cake   67

Coconut Cloud Cake   69

Cranberry-Apple Upside-Down Cake   71

Pistachio Semolina Honey Cake   73

Café au Lait Chocolate Cake   74

Golden Ricotta Cheesecake   77

Nutmeg Sweet-Potato Cake   78

Pumpkin Spice Cake   80

Maple Walnut Cake   83

Brown-Sugar Pound Cake   85

Lemon Cakes with Berry Salsa   86

Four-Layer Gingerbread Cake   89

Pound Cake   91

Chocolate Roulade   92

Chocolate Cream Cakes   94

Flourless Chocolate Cake   97

Fresh Berry Shortcake   98

Summer Upside-Down Cake   100

Lemon-Blackberry Cake   103

Apple Bundt Cake   105

Pumpkin-Date Spice Cupcakes   106

Coconut Hummingbird Cake   109

Strawberry Savarin   110

Frozen Raspberry Layer Cake   112

Cinnamon Pear Torte   115

Chocolate Espresso Torte   116

Stacked Applesauce Cake   119

Grandma Stonesifer's Spice Cake   121

Measurement Conversion Chart   123

Photography Credits   125

Index   127

If you think back to some of your favorite celebrations, chances are many of them involved a special—and delicious—cake. After all, what would a birthday, graduation, wedding, promotion, homecoming, farewell, or anniversary be without fanciful decorations or a flurry of lighted candles flickering atop a lovingly made cake? And some of my most fondly remembered moments are those in which a warm slice of fragrant cake and a cold glass of milk are ready and waiting—on just an ordinary day. These are the cakes that stay with us for a lifetime—grandmother's snack cake, Aunt Annie's pound cake, and a best friend's famous coconut cupcakes.

During my years at *Country Living*, I've had the pleasure of tasting dozens of mouth-watering cakes, from elegant tortes and cheesecakes to playful children's birthday cakes and beloved classic cakes. We've collected fifty of the most tempting standouts here—there's one for every milestone occasion—with the hope that you will enjoy them not just on the red-letter days, but on many of the others in between, too.

—Nancy Soriano,
Editor-in-Chief, *Country Living*

When it comes to celebrating one of life's special moments, nothing does it better than a beautifully presented homemade cake. Whether the occasion is a birthday, bar or bat mitzvah, graduation, marriage, or anniversary, a cake marks an occasion in a way that nothing else can. And even though we have come to expect a cake at these times, it is always anticipated and always welcome and has been so throughout the years. Part of a cake's charm is perhaps that we often go to great lengths to bake up a beloved flavor, frost it with patience and care, and summon every ounce of creativity to decorate it impressively. Ask almost anyone what they remember most fondly about their childhood, and chances are an early birthday, when luminous candles atop a thickly frosted cake cast a golden glow and made them feel like they were floating on air, will be recalled. These magical moments, often marked by pomp and circumstance, become permanently etched in our memories as markers of cherished times in our lives.

Baking—and eating—cake should not be reserved for special occasions, however. A delicious slice of cake can turn the most mundane day into a dazzling one. Imagine the love a child feels when there is a favorite spicy apple snack cake, warm from the oven, waiting for him at home after a long day at school. Or picture the smile on your spouse's face when you set down a thick slice of adored angel food cake after the dinner dishes have been cleared. The aroma of Toasted Coconut Coffee Cake is guaranteed to charm even the most reluctant sleepyhead out of bed and into the kitchen. When a cake comes as a complete surprise, the impact is everlasting.

Whenever you feel the urge to celebrate a snow day off from school, a victory on the ball field, or a poignant recital performance, baking a cake is one of the most fulfilling and thoughtful ways to express this sentiment. In fact, when a cake is part of the menu, it automatically becomes a bit of a celebration. And when a tiered confection is set proudly on a pretty cake stand, there's no mistaking that the occasion is special—that's the beauty of cake. In *Great Cakes,* we offer countless flavor combinations, presentations, and decorations to entice you into the kitchen to start baking.

There is something for everyone in this impressive collection of *Country Living's* best cake recipes, including a cake for every celebration and season. You'll find birthday cakes for little kids and grown-ups alike, such as a colorful Big-Top Carnival Cake for young ones in love with the

circus as well as a sophisticated Stacked Applesauce Cake cake for Mom or Dad. For impromptu gatherings, there are simple-to-prepare—yet no less enchanting—confections, including an Easy Chocolate Party Cake with Fudgy Cream Cheese Frosting and a Frozen Raspberry Layer Cake. You can bake year-round, beginning in the spring with Banana-Caramel Cake, which is frosted and filled with scrumptious caramel icing. Then sail right into summer with Summer Upside-Down Cake, which has a vanilla batter studded with juicy ripe fruit: cherries and apricots or raspberries, peaches and nectarines. In the fall, what could be more satisfying after an afternoon of leaf raking than a warm slice of Apple Bundt Cake and a cup of tea? And on a snowy winter's morning, there's nothing more comforting than a slice of Brown Sugar Pound Cake and a mug of steaming hot coffee. We've included classic favorites in this eclectic collection, too, because they always please. There's German Chocolate Cake, our version of Red Velvet Cake and, of course, a Flourless Chocolate Cake, which is practically foolproof and will make you look like an expert baker, even if you're just a beginner.

Unlike making soup, roasting vegetables, or putting together a tossed salad, baking a cake is an exact science. There is little room for substitutions, not to mention inaccurate measurements. While it would be nice to be able to follow recipes the way our grandmothers did by using "a pinch of this, a dash of that, and butter the size of a walnut" to achieve the same excellent results time after time, it's important to follow standardized recipes. We recommend that you begin baking the way professionals do, by getting organized. Read the recipe at least once through before you start, then assemble your ingredients and equipment. You will find that simple cakes, such as Grandma Stonesifer's Spice Cake and our Flourless Chocolate Cake, can be made within hours if you begin this way. For more elaborate confections that contain several components, such as cake, filling, frosting, and decoration, plan on making them in stages so that on the day you serve the cake, all you have to do is assemble and frost it. The Four-Layer Gingerbread Cake, Chocolate Roulade, and classic Red Velvet Cake are good examples of cakes that are best made in steps.

Ingredients

As in all baking, using the best—and freshest—ingredients available makes the difference between so-so and spectacular cakes. The basic ingredients, flour, eggs, sweeteners, and leaveners, should all be purchased fresh, from a grocer whose supply turns over quickly.

ALL-PURPOSE FLOUR * Most cakes in this book call for all-purpose flour, which is used in cakes that don't need to rise excessively high such as pound cake. All-purpose flour is made from a mix of soft and hard wheats and produces cakes with a tender crumb. All-purpose flour is available bleached and unbleached. You can use either in our recipes. The bleaching process simply whitens the flour and makes it slightly easier to absorb liquids.

CAKE FLOUR * Run one hand through some cake flour and the other through all-purpose, and you will instantly feel the difference. Cake flour is made solely from soft wheat and has a lower protein content than all-purpose flour. It is best for delicate cakes, such as angel food and sponge cakes. While it is not recommended to substitute all-purpose for cake flour when a recipe calls for it, you may need to in a pinch. For every cup of cake flour, use ¾ cup plus 2 tablespoons of all-purpose flour.

GRANULATED SUGAR * Many of our cakes call for granulated sugar. It can be made from cane sugar or sugar beets. Both make fine-quality sugar that works well in baking.

BROWN SUGAR * This type of sugar adds flavor and moisture to cake. It is made from refined white sugar and molasses. Light and dark brown sugar can usually be used interchangeably, though dark brown sugar contains a bit more molasses and will produce a slightly denser cake.

CONFECTIONERS' SUGAR * This sweetener, which feels a bit like cornstarch, actually contains a small percentage of cornstarch, which prevents clumping. Confectioners' sugar is very finely ground granulated sugar (confectioners' sugar and granulated sugar are not interchangeable). It is often used to decorate cakes rather than to sweeten them. Tap the sugar through a fine mesh strainer or sieve to give a cake a "dusted" look.

HONEY * There are literally hundreds of different flavors of honey. Each depends on the flower the nectar was gathered from. The honey you use is a matter of personal taste; dark honeys, like brown sugar, impart a deeper, richer taste than lighter varieties.

BAKING POWDER * A leavener is what makes cakes rise. Double-acting baking powder releases gas in two stages. It is first released when it is mixed into a liquid, then it rises a second time from the heat of the oven. It is made from a combination of baking soda, and acid, a moisture absorber.

BAKING SODA * Also known as bicarbonate of soda, baking soda is a chemical leavener that neutralizes acidic ingredients, such as chocolate, pumpkin, buttermilk, and yogurt. It is often used in combination with baking powder.

BUTTER * Fresh, good-quality butter will result in a superior cake, so seek out the best you can find and afford. To test butter for freshness, scrape away a piece from the surface and compare the color of the outside to the inside. If the outside is darker, the butter has oxidized—it is essentially rancid. Do not use it. For the best results, always soften butter at room temperature before using it in cakes.

MILK * Whole milk is used in our recipes.

CREAM * Use whipping cream that is 36 percent butterfat in recipes that call for heavy cream. To make perfectly peaked whipped cream, chill the bowl, cream, and beaters before beginning to whip it. You can slide the whole thing—the bowl of cream with the whisk in it—right into the freezer to chill for 15 to 20 minutes. To avoid overbeating, whisk cream until just firm enough to spread; if you continue to beat much beyond this point, the cream will separate.

SOUR CREAM * Use the full-fat variety for the most luscious flavor.

CREAM CHEESE * Use the full-fat variety. This soft, unripened cheese adds both a slight tang and richness to cakes. Make it easier to work with by allowing it to soften at room temperature first.

MASCARPONE * A rich Italian cream cheese with a spreadable texture, mascarpone is often lightly sweetened and spread between the layers of a cake.

RICOTTA * This mild-tasting, milky Italian curd cheese makes a deliciously smooth and airy cheesecake. Fresh ricotta can often be found at good Italian delis and specialty food stores; use it if it is available to you.

Equipment

Once you've assembled your ingredients, pull together all of the equipment you're going to need to make your cake. Using the right equipment and the correct-size pan will help to ensure that your cake bakes up perfectly in the right amount of time. Here's a rundown of the equipment used to prepare the cakes in this collection:

MIXER * If you're an avid baker, you likely own a heavy-duty stand mixer with a flat paddle (good for general mixing and firm batters) and whisk (performs like a hand whisk but with far less work!) attachments. A hand mixer will do the job, too, though it will likely not be able to handle some very dense, firm mixtures.

FOOD PROCESSOR * This machine is an indispensable time saver for chopping or finely grinding nuts.

THERMOMETERS * Instant-read and candy thermometers are must-have items when it comes to knowing the exact temperature of cooked frostings and certain types of meringues.

SPATULAS * You'll need two kinds: a wide pancake turner for transferring cakes to cooling racks and onto serving dishes and a small and large offset spatula for spreading frosting.

BAKING PANS * Using the correct-size baking pan is critical to the success of a cake. If you have the following in your pantry, you can make any cake in this book:

Two sets each of 8-, 9-, 10-, and 12-inch round pans that are 2 inches deep.
9- by 5- by 3-inch loaf pan
8½- by 4½- by 2¾-inch loaf pan
12-cup Bundt pan
10-inch tube pan with a removable bottom
7-, 9-, and 10-inch springform pans
Four 5- by 2½-inch mini loaf pans
Standard muffin pans
Two 15½- by 10½- by 1-inch jelly-roll pans
Four 9-inch square baking pans
Baking sheet
6-cup Kugelhof or Bundt pan
10-inch ring mold
Five 6-ounce ramekins
10-inch cast-iron skillet

COOLING RACKS ∗ You will need two—sometimes three—for the recipes. Most cakes are left in their pans for 10 minutes before being inverted onto wire racks to cool completely. If a cake is removed from its pan while too hot, it may fall apart.

MEASURING EQUIPMENT ∗ Accurate measuring is crucial to the success of any cake. To measure dry ingredients, use a standard set of nested measures in graduations of ¼-, ⅓-, ½-, and 1-cup. Measure flour using the dip-and-level method: Dip the measuring cup into the flour and level it with the flat side of a knife.

To measure liquid ingredients, use glass or clear plastic spouted measuring cups. Fill the cup so that it reaches the top of the line for the reading you need. Set the glass on a level surface, preferably at eye level (if it's on a low counter, lean down to look at the cup at eye level).

A set of measuring spoons can be used for liquids and dry ingredients. Scoop a dry ingredient (such as baking powder) into the spoon and level with the flat side of a knife. For wet ingredients (such as vanilla), pour them directly into the spoon, away from the batter so any overflow doesn't fall into the batter.

Twelve Tips for Better Baking

Here are some baking tips that will help any novice baker feel right at home in the kitchen.

1 ∗ Always read a recipe thoroughly before starting. Note the oven temperature, baking time, and any special equipment you may need. Before starting, gather together all the ingredients called for in the recipe and don't take any shortcuts.

2 ∗ Pay close attention to recipe ingredients. If large eggs are called for, don't use jumbo, medium, or small. The type of flour specified, milk (whole, skim, or buttermilk), and sugar (dark brown, light brown, granulated, or confectioners') can make a big difference in the final product.

3 ∗ Measure ingredients accurately. To measure dry ingredients, start by stirring the ingredient in its container with a fork or whisk to aerate it, then dip the measure to scoop up the ingredient. Level the cup off with a straightedge, such as a narrow spatula or the flat side of a knife, over the container, then transfer the ingredient to the bowl or sifter. To measure liquids properly, place the measuring cup on a flat surface, add the liquid, then check the accuracy of the amount at eye level.

4 ∗ Don't be tempted to open the oven door too soon to peek at what's baking. A sudden drop in temperature can ruin cookies or cakes; it's important to maintain even heat during baking. When you do open the oven door, open it all the way, until it is parallel to the floor; a door opened only part way can spring back up and burn your arms.

5 ✷ Oven thermostats vary: Use an oven thermometer to be sure your oven is at the proper temperature. Most cakes are baked on the middle rack, where the temperature is most even, though some tall cakes (such as angel food) are often baked in the lower third of the oven so that the middle of the cake is in the center of the oven. The bottom is closer to the heat source and heat rises to the top. Rotate cake pans from the bottom rack to the middle or from the back to the front of the shelves to ensure even baking.

6 ✷ To test for doneness, insert a wooden toothpick or a metal cake tester. It should come out clean. The cake should also spring back when pressed lightly in the center even before it is done. If a cake is underbaked, it will contain gummy spots instead of a fine crumb throughout.

7 ✷ Be careful while working around hot surfaces, such as burners, ovens, and hot pans. Always be sure to use long dry oven mitts or hot pads.

8 ✷ Allow baked goods to cool completely when a recipe suggests doing so, even if you're anxious to taste the fruits of your labor. Set hot baking sheets or cake pans on a heatproof surface, such as wire racks, cutting boards, or trivets, then transfer the warm cookies or cake to wire racks set over waxed paper to finish cooling.

9 ✷ Take the chill off: For smooth, silky batter every time, make sure batter ingredients are at room temperature—unless otherwise specified. If you are in a hurry or forget to remove them from the refrigerator ahead of time, you can warm eggs (still in their shell) by placing them in a bowl of hot tap water. Liquids can be slightly warmed on the stovetop or in the microwave oven.

10 ✷ Use a generous amount of frosting to build up a good layer. Trying to spread a skimpy amount of frosting means pressing against the sides and getting crumbs into the frosting.

11 ✷ Keep your cake plate or stand neat by placing waxed paper strips all along the edge of the cake plate, tucking them just underneath the cake. Frost the cake, then carefully pull away the paper strips to reveal a picture perfect cake.

12 ✷ Use a thin, sharp blade to cut a frosted cake. When the blade reaches the bottom of the cake, wiggle it slightly to ensure that the slice is free and pull the blade straight out without lifting it back up through the cake. Then use a cake server to slip out the cake slice. Wipe the knife with a damp cloth after cutting each slice to keep the crumbs and frosting from becoming messy.

RECIPES

German Chocolate Cake

This beloved American cake is named after Samuel German, who developed
German's sweet baking chocolate. For a traditional presentation, spread the pecan and coconut filling
over each layer and leave the sides unfrosted. * MAKES 16 SERVINGS (ONE 8-INCH 3-LAYER CAKE)

1/2 cup boiling water

4 ounces German's Chocolate,
    coarsely chopped

2 cups all-purpose flour

1/4 cup unsweetened cocoa

1 teaspoon baking soda

1 teaspoon salt

1 cup unsalted butter (2 sticks), softened

2 cups sugar

4 large eggs, separated, at room
    temperature

1 teaspoon vanilla extract

1 cup buttermilk

Coconut-Pecan Filling (recipe follows)

① MAKE THE BATTER: Preheat the oven to 350°F. Lightly coat three 8-inch cake pans with butter. Dust with flour and tap out any excess. Set aside. Pour the boiling water over the German's Chocolate in a medium bowl. Stir until smooth and set aside. Combine the flour, cocoa, baking soda, and salt in another medium bowl. Set aside. Beat the butter and sugar in a large bowl using a mixer set on medium-high speed, until very light—about 5 minutes. Add the egg yolks, one at a time, beating well after each addition. Reduce the mixer speed to low and add the chocolate mixture and vanilla. Add the flour mixture by thirds, alternating with the buttermilk and ending with the dry ingredients, mixing just until the batter is smooth. Beat the egg whites in a clean medium bowl with clean beaters until they form soft peaks. Gently fold 1/2 cup of the beaten whites into the batter. Fold the remaining whites into the batter until blended.

② BAKE THE CAKE: Divide the batter equally between the prepared pans and spread evenly. Bake until a tester inserted into the center of each cake layer comes out clean—30 to 35 minutes. Cool in the pans on wire racks for 15 minutes. Use a knife to loosen the cake layers from the sides of the pan and invert onto the wire racks to cool completely.

③ ASSEMBLE THE CAKE: Place a cake layer on a cake plate and top with one third of the Coconut-Pecan Filling. Repeat with the remaining layers and filling. Serve or store in an airtight container at room temperature.

Coconut-Pecan Filling

1 cup sugar

1 12-ounce can evaporated milk

1/2 cup unsalted butter (1 stick)

3 large egg yolks

1 teaspoon vanilla extract

1 7-ounce package sweetened flaked
    coconut

1 1/2 cups chopped pecans

MAKE THE FILLING: Combine the sugar, evaporated milk, butter, egg yolks, and vanilla in a medium saucepan. Cook over medium heat, stirring constantly, until the mixture thickens—about 10 minutes. Stir in the coconut and pecans. Transfer to a bowl and cool to room temperature, stirring occasionally, before using to frost the cake.

NUTRITION INFORMATION PER SERVING—PROTEIN: 7.7 G; FAT: 35.5 G; CARBOHYDRATE: 65.4 G; FIBER: 2.4 G; SODIUM: 304 MG; CHOLESTEROL: 147 MG; CALORIES: 592.

Carrot Pistachio Cake and Cupcakes

This dried-apricot-and-pistachio–studded carrot cake bakes up into two layers and cupcakes—
all from one recipe. Freeze the cake so it is on hand for an impromptu gathering and enjoy the cupcakes
as a tasty, portable dessert. Frost the cooled cakes or cupcakes with your favorite icing, if desired.

✳ MAKES 12 SERVINGS (TWO 8-INCH ROUND CAKE LAYERS AND 8 CUPCAKES)

3 cups all-purpose flour

1 1/2 cups granulated sugar

1/2 cup firmly packed dark brown sugar

1 tablespoon baking soda

2 teaspoons baking powder

1 1/2 teaspoons salt

1 1/2 teaspoons ground cinnamon

1 teaspoon freshly grated nutmeg

1/2 teaspoon allspice

3 cups grated carrots

1 1/2 cups chopped dried apricots

1 1/2 cups chopped pistachios

4 large eggs

1 1/2 cups mild olive oil

1/2 cup milk

2 tablespoons vanilla extract

① MAKE THE BATTER: Preheat the oven to 350°F. Butter two 8-inch cake pans, line an 8-cup muffin pan with paper liners, and set aside. Combine the flour, sugars, baking soda, baking powder, salt, cinnamon, nutmeg, and allspice in a large bowl. Add the carrots, apricots, and pistachios to the flour mixture, toss until mixed, and set aside. Whisk the eggs, olive oil, milk, and vanilla together in a medium bowl and add to the flour mixture. Stir until just combined.

② BAKE THE CAKES AND CUPCAKES: Spoon 3 cups batter into each prepared pan and ¼ cup batter into each lined muffin cup. Bake until a tester inserted into the center of each layer comes out clean—about 20 minutes for the cupcakes and 40 minutes for the cake layers. Transfer the cupcakes to a wire rack and cool completely. Cool the cakes in the pans on wire racks for 20 minutes. Use a knife to loosen the cake layers from the sides of the pans and invert onto the wire racks to cool completely. If freezing, skip to Step 3. Frost with your favorite icing.

③ TO FREEZE: Double-wrap the cake layers in plastic wrap or place each one in a large resealable plastic bag, pressing out the excess air. Place the cupcakes in an airtight container and freeze for up to 2 months.

✳ Freezing Cake ✳

A festive cake is always an impressive way to celebrate a special occasion—it's also a big job from start to finish. But with a supply of prebaked fresh-frozen layers in your freezer you can have your cake whenever you please. Start by dividing the work into tasks: baking and freezing; thawing and frosting. To freeze, double-wrap each cake layer in plastic wrap or place each one in a large resealable plastic bag, removing the excess air. Place cupcakes in a plastic container with an airtight lid. Both cake layers and cupcakes can be frozen for up to 2 months.

It is also possible to freeze cakes that are frosted with buttercream. This type of frosting freezes without making the cake soggy. If, however, you prefer egg white–based or cream-cheese icings, freeze the cake layers separately, make the icing fresh, and frost the layers once they are thawed.

NUTRITION INFORMATION PER CUPCAKE OR 1/12 SLICE CAKE—PROTEIN: 7 G; FAT: 28 G; CARBOHYDRATE: 54.4 G;
FIBER: 3.7 G; SODIUM: 524 MG; CHOLESTEROL: 53 MG; CALORIES: 488.

Grandma's Applesauce Cake

An unusual combination of warm and spicy flavors makes this applesauce cake
one of the best. A generous amount of applesauce keeps the cake very moist while the addition
of cocoa powder and brewed coffee adds depth of flavor. ✱ MAKES 10 SERVINGS

2 cups all-purpose flour

1/2 cup unsweetened cocoa

1 1/2 teaspoons ground cinnamon

1 teaspoon ground allspice

1 teaspoon baking powder

1 teaspoon baking soda

1/2 teaspoon salt

1/4 teaspoon ground cloves

1/2 cup butter (1 stick), softened

1 1/2 cups firmly packed dark brown sugar

2 large eggs

1 1/2 cups applesauce

3/4 cup strongly brewed hot coffee

1 1/2 cups dark raisins

3/4 cup chopped walnuts

2 cups confectioners' sugar

① MAKE THE BATTER: Preheat the oven to 350ºF. Lightly butter a 6-cup Kugelhopf or Bundt pan. Dust with flour and tap out any excess. Set aside. Combine the flour, 1/4 cup of the cocoa powder, cinnamon, allspice, baking powder, baking soda, salt, and cloves in a large bowl and set aside. Beat the butter and brown sugar in a large bowl using a mixer set on medium-high speed until light and fluffy. Add the eggs, one at a time, beating just until incorporated. Reduce the mixer speed to low and add the flour mixture by thirds, alternating with the applesauce and ending with the dry ingredients. Scrape down the sides of the bowl and increase the mixer speed to medium. Quickly add 1/2 cup of the hot coffee, beating until thoroughly combined—about 30 seconds. Fold in the raisins and walnuts.

② BAKE THE CAKE: Pour the batter into the prepared pan and spread evenly. Bake until a tester inserted into the center of the cake comes out clean—40 to 45 minutes. Cool in the pan on a wire rack until slightly warm. Use a knife to loosen the cake from the edges of the pan and invert the cake onto the wire rack to cool completely.

③ GLAZE THE CAKE: Sift the confectioners' sugar and remaining cocoa together into a medium bowl. Make a well in the center and quickly pour in the remaining hot coffee. Whisk until well blended and smooth. Pour the glaze over the top of the cake, allowing it to soak in. Serve immediately. Store at room temperature for up to 3 days.

NUTRITION INFORMATION PER SERVING—PROTEIN: 7.9 G; FAT: 16.6 G; CARBOHYDRATE: 85.7 G; FIBER: 3.9 G; SODIUM: 309 MG; CHOLESTEROL: 67.4 MG; CALORIES: 494.

Berry-Dotted Angel Food Cake

Here a splash of color is added to a basic angel food cake by baking red, black, and golden raspberries into the batter. The berries create a polka dot design and add a burst of fresh fruit flavor to every bite. Garnish each slice with some mixed berries, if desired. ✷ MAKES 12 SERVINGS

1 cup plus 1 tablespoon cake flour

1¼ cups sugar

1 tablespoon cornstarch

³/₄ teaspoon salt

12 large egg whites (about 1¹/₃ cups), at room temperature

1 teaspoon cream of tartar

1¹/₂ teaspoons vanilla extract

1¹/₂ cups small firm red, black, and golden raspberries

① MAKE THE BATTER: Preheat the oven to 350°F. Combine 1 cup cake flour, ½ cup sugar, cornstarch, and salt in a large bowl. Sift together twice and set aside. Combine the egg whites and cream of tartar in a large bowl and beat using a mixer set on low speed until foamy—about 3 minutes. Add the remaining sugar and vanilla and increase the speed to medium-high. Beat until the egg whites form stiff peaks. Do not overbeat. Set aside.

② BAKE THE CAKE: Sift one third of the reserved flour mixture over the beaten egg whites and gently fold together. Sift another third of the flour on top and fold in. Add the berries in an even layer and sift the remaining flour over the berries. Fold gently until combined. Gently scrape the batter into an ungreased 10-inch tube pan and spread evenly. Bake in the lower third of the oven until the cake is golden brown and springs back when lightly touched—40 to 50 minutes. Invert the cake and cool completely—about 1½ hours. Use a knife to loosen the cake from the sides and center tube of the pan and invert onto a cake plate. Store at room temperature for up to 2 days.

✷ Light and Airy ✷

To achieve a light, airy angel food cake every time, follow these basic steps: Avoid overbeating the egg whites—they become dry and grainy, making it hard to fold in the flour; never oil the cake pan—the batter needs to "grab" the pan as it rises in order to reach maximum height; finally, cool the cake inverted, either over a tall narrow-necked bottle or resting on four tall inverted glasses, until it is completely cool.

NUTRITION INFORMATION PER SERVING—PROTEIN: 4.4 G; FAT: .2 G; CARBOHYDRATE: 31 G; FIBER: 1 G; SODIUM: 189 MG; CHOLESTEROL: 0; CALORIES: 142.

Pear Upside-Down Cake

The surprise ingredient in this batter is stone-ground cornmeal, which lends a crunchy texture to the luscious pears and caramelized sugar. This dessert comes to us from Alyssa Linder, former pastry chef at the New York City restaurant Remi. Alyssa says a Teflon-coated cake pan will work just as well as the springform pan we used. * MAKES 10 SERVINGS (ONE 8-INCH CAKE)

1³/₄ cups sugar

6 tablespoons unsalted butter

2 Bartlett pears, peeled, one cut crosswise into ¹/₄-inch-thick slices and the other cut into ¹/₂-inch-thick wedges

¹/₄ cup plus 2 tablespoons all-purpose flour

¹/₄ cup plus 1 tablespoon cornmeal

¹/₂ teaspoon baking powder

¹/₄ teaspoon salt

2 large eggs

4 large egg yolks

① MAKE THE CARAMEL: Preheat the oven to 325°F. Put 1 cup of the sugar in a small saucepan over medium-high heat and cook until the sugar liquefies and becomes amber in color. Stir in 2 tablespoons of the butter until combined and pour the caramel into an ungreased 8-inch springform cake pan, tilting the pan to coat the bottom evenly. Arrange the pear slices in a single layer on top of the caramel and set aside.

② MAKE THE CAKE BATTER: Sift the flour, cornmeal, baking powder, and salt together into a medium bowl and set aside. Beat the remaining butter and sugar in the large bowl of a mixer set on medium-high speed until light and fluffy—about 5 minutes. Add the eggs and egg yolks, one at a time, beating well after each addition. Reduce the mixer speed to low, add the dry ingredients, and mix just until combined.

③ BAKE THE CAKE: Gently spread the batter evenly over the pears and bake until a tester inserted into the center of the cake comes out clean—about 45 minutes. Cool slightly and remove the pan rim. Invert the cake onto a serving plate and remove the pan base. Serve warm or at room temperature.

NUTRITION INFORMATION PER SERVING—PROTEIN: 3.4 G; FAT: 10.3 G; CARBOHYDRATE: 46.8 G; FIBER: 1.2 G; SODIUM: 90.5 MG; CHOLESTEROL: 146 MG; CALORIES: 286.

Blueberry Hill Cheesecake

Named after the famed inn in Vermont, this remarkably creamy confection takes a bit of patience to make but is well worth the time spent. The secret to the cake's texture is that the batter is beaten for a full 30 minutes. Use a standing mixer or let guests pitch in. The result—the perfect cake to serve at the end of a summer meal. ✻ MAKES 12 SERVINGS (ONE 9-INCH CAKE)

4 8-ounce packages cream cheese, softened
1¹/₂ cups sugar
4 large eggs
2 teaspoons vanilla extract
2 teaspoons fresh lemon juice
1 cup graham cracker crumbs
   (about 6 rectangular graham crackers)
¹/₂ cup unsalted butter (1 stick), melted
2 cups Glacéed Blueberries (recipe follows)

① MAKE THE BATTER: Beat the cream cheese, sugar, eggs, vanilla, and lemon juice in a large bowl using a mixer set on low speed until very smooth—about 30 minutes.

② BAKE THE CHEESECAKE: Preheat the oven to 350°F. Combine the graham cracker crumbs and melted butter in a small bowl and firmly press into the bottom of a 9-inch springform pan. Pour the batter into the prepared pan and spread evenly. Bake until a tester inserted into the center of the cake comes out clean—about 1 hour. Cool completely in the pan on a wire rack. Use a knife to loosen the cake from the sides of the pan and remove the pan rim. Refrigerate for at least 5 hours or overnight. Spoon the Glacéed Blueberries over the top of the cheesecake and drizzle the remaining berry syrup over the sides of the cake. Store refrigerated for up to 4 days.

Glacéed Blueberries

¹/₂ cup red-currant jelly
1¹/₂ tablespoons crème de cassis
2 cups fresh blueberries

COOK THE BLUEBERRIES: Heat the jelly in a glass measuring cup in the microwave until melted—about 30 seconds—or in a small saucepan set over medium-low heat until liquefied. Stir in the crème de cassis. Combine the blueberries and jelly in a large bowl and gently toss until the berries are coated. Refrigerate in covered container up to 3 days.

NUTRITION INFORMATION PER SERVING OF CHEESECAKE WITHOUT GLACÉED BLUEBERRIES—PROTEIN: 8.6 G; FAT: 36.6 G; CARBOHYDRATE: 45.5 G; FIBER: 1 G; SODIUM: 295 MG; CHOLESTEROL: 175 MG; CALORIES: 537.

NUTRITION INFORMATION PER ¼-CUP SERVING OF GLACÉED BLUEBERRIES—PROTEIN: .4 G; FAT: .2 G; CARBOHYDRATE: 19.2 G; FIBER: 1.2 G; SODIUM: 10.3 MG; CHOLESTEROL: 0; CALORIES: 78.

Easy Chocolate Party Cake

No wonder this is one of our most beloved cakes as it is so simple to prepare.
It's often called a "dump" cake, since all of the ingredients are easily combined in one bowl
and beaten into a smooth batter. ✳ MAKES 16 SERVINGS (ONE 8-INCH 2-LAYER CAKE)

2 cups all-purpose flour

2/3 cup granulated sugar

2/3 cup firmly packed dark brown sugar

1/2 cup unsweetened cocoa

1 1/2 cups whole milk

3/4 cup butter (1 1/2 sticks), softened

3 large eggs

2 teaspoons vanilla extract

1 teaspoon baking powder

1 teaspoon baking soda

1/2 teaspoon salt

Fudgy Cream-Cheese Frosting
(recipe follows)

① MAKE THE BATTER: Preheat the oven to 350°F. Lightly butter two 8-inch cake pans. Dust with flour and tap out any excess. Set aside. Combine the flour, sugars, cocoa, milk, butter, eggs, vanilla, baking powder, baking soda, and salt in a large bowl using a mixer set on low speed, until blended. Increase the mixer speed to medium and continue to beat until the batter is smooth—about 3 more minutes.

② BAKE THE CAKE: Divide the batter equally between the prepared pans and spread evenly. Bake until the tops of the cakes spring back when lightly touched. Cool in the cake pans on wire racks for 10 minutes. Use a knife to loosen the cake layers from the sides of the pans and invert the cake layers onto the wire racks to cool completely.

③ FROST THE CAKE: Use a serrated knife to level the tops of the cake layers, if necessary. Line the edges of a cake plate with 3-inch-wide strips of waxed or parchment paper and place a cake layer, trimmed side down, on top. Place 1/2 cup Fudgy Cream-Cheese Frosting on top of the layer and spread evenly. Place the second layer, trimmed side down, on top of the first and cover the top and sides with the remaining icing. Remove the paper strips and serve. Store refrigerated for up to 4 days.

Fudgy Cream-Cheese Frosting

1 8-ounce package cream cheese, softened

1/4 cup butter (1/2 stick), softened

3 tablespoons whole milk

3 cups sifted confectioners' sugar

2/3 cup unsweetened cocoa

1/8 teaspoon salt

1 1/2 teaspoons vanilla extract

MAKE THE ICING: Beat the cream cheese, butter, and milk in a medium bowl using a mixer set on medium speed until smooth. Add the confectioners' sugar, cocoa, and salt and continue to beat until blended. Reduce the mixer speed to low, add the vanilla, and beat just until smooth. Cover and refrigerate for at least 30 minutes before using.

NUTRITION INFORMATION PER SERVING—PROTEIN: 8.1 G; FAT: 25.7 G; CARBOHYDRATE: 64.8 G;
FIBER: 3.5 G; SODIUM: 350 MG; CHOLESTEROL: 120 MG; CALORIES: 503.

"Hot" Chocolate Cake

Aptly named for the pairing of rich cocoa, bittersweet chocolate, and a hint of cayenne pepper, this "Hot" Chocolate Cake is a dark, rich, and welcome treat on a chilly winter's day.

✱ MAKES 12 SERVINGS (ONE 9-INCH CAKE)

1/4 cup plus 1 tablespoon unsweetened cocoa

1 cup all-purpose flour

1/2 teaspoon baking powder

1/2 teaspoon salt

1/4 teaspoon ground cinnamon

1/4 teaspoon cayenne pepper

8 ounces bittersweet chocolate, chopped

1/2 cup plus 2 tablespoons unsalted butter (1 stick plus 2 tablespoons)

4 large eggs

1/2 cup granulated sugar

1/3 cup firmly packed dark brown sugar

1 teaspoon vanilla extract

① MAKE THE BATTER: Preheat the oven to 350°F. Butter a 9-inch cake pan. Line the bottom with parchment paper and butter the paper. Dust with the 1 tablespoon cocoa and tap out any excess. Set aside. Sift the flour, the 1/4 cup cocoa, baking powder, salt, cinnamon, and cayenne together into a medium bowl and set aside. In a double boiler over simmering water, melt 6 ounces of the chocolate and the butter. Remove from the heat and set aside. Beat the eggs and sugars together in a large bowl using a mixer set on medium-high speed until the mixture thickens and increases in volume—about 5 minutes. Reduce the mixer speed to low, add the chocolate mixture and vanilla, and beat until combined. Gradually add the flour mixture and beat until the batter is smooth.

② BAKE THE CAKE: Pour the batter into the prepared pan and spread evenly. Bake until the cake springs back when lightly touched in the center—30 to 40 minutes. Cool in the cake pan on a wire rack for 20 minutes. Use a knife to loosen the cake from the sides of the pan and invert the cake onto the wire rack. Remove the parchment paper and cool completely.

③ GLAZE THE CAKE: Transfer the cake to a serving plate. Melt the remaining bittersweet chocolate and drizzle over the top of the cake. Store at room temperature for up to 3 days.

NUTRITION INFORMATION PER SERVING—PROTEIN: 5.1 G; FAT: 19.1 G; CARBOHYDRATE: 30.3 G; FIBER: 1.6 G; SODIUM: 130 MG; CHOLESTEROL: 96.9 MG; CALORIES: 290.

Chocolate Peanut Cheesecake

How about a delectable cheesecake you can prepare in less than 30 minutes? Making this smooth-as-silk cheesecake topped with toasted peanuts and crunchy crumbled chocolate wafer cookies is as easy as can be: Just combine an indulgent combination of peanut butter, bittersweet chocolate, and cream in a pressure cooker and 30 minutes later, it's ready to be chilled. ✳ MAKES 8 SERVINGS (ONE 7-INCH CAKE)

1/4 cup turbinado (coarse) sugar

1 8-ounce package cream cheese, softened

1 cup plus 3 tablespoons creamy peanut
    butter

1/2 cup confectioners' sugar, sifted

1/4 cup firmly packed light brown sugar

2 tablespoons cornstarch

3 large eggs

1/4 cup sour cream

1 teaspoon vanilla extract

8 ounces good-quality bittersweet
    chocolate, melted and cooled

2/3 cup chopped toasted peanuts

4 1/2 ounces chocolate wafers, crushed

1/4 cup butter (1/2 stick), melted

1/8 teaspoon salt

① MAKE THE BATTER: Lightly butter a 7-inch springform pan, coat it with the turbinado sugar. Tightly wrap the outside of the pan with aluminum foil to prevent any water seepage. Set aside. Beat the cream cheese and the 1 cup of the peanut butter in a medium bowl using a mixer set on low speed, until combined. Beat in the sugars and cornstarch. Beat in the eggs, one at a time, beating well after each addition. Add the sour cream and vanilla and beat until incorporated. Add the melted chocolate and mix well.

② PREPARE THE CAKE: Pour the batter into the prepared pan and spread evenly. Place two sheets of paper toweling across the top of the pan and cover with 1 sheet of foil. Create a foil handle by scrunching a 32-inch-long piece of foil. Place it under the pan, then bring up each side to create a handle.

③ COOK THE CAKE: Place the pressure cooker's trivet accessory in the bottom of the pan and add 2 cups water. Using the foil handle, lower the cake pan into the pressure cooker. Seal the pressure cooker lid and bring the cooker to high pressure. Reduce the heat just enough to maintain high pressure and cook for 22 minutes. Quick-release the pressure and carefully remove the lid. Lift out the cake pan and place on a wire rack to cool completely. Refrigerate overnight.

④ TOP THE CAKE: Combine the peanuts, chocolate-wafer crumbs, melted butter, and salt in a small bowl. Warm the remaining peanut butter to soften and spread it over the top of the cake. Top with peanut and chocolate-wafer mixture. Store refrigerated for up to 4 days.

NUTRITION INFORMATION PER SERVING—PROTEIN: 21.5 G; FAT: 58.2 G; CARBOHYDRATE: 53.2 G; FIBER: 4.2 G; SODIUM: 319 MG; CHOLESTEROL: 133 MG; CALORIES: 767.

Big-Top Carnival Cake

Sure to be a hit with the kids, this circus-themed moist chocolate cake is guaranteed to be a showstopper at your next birthday party. ✳ MAKES 12 SERVINGS (ONE 8-INCH 2-LAYER CAKE)

1 cup boiling water

1 cup unsweetened cocoa

¹/₂ cup buttermilk

1³/₄ cups all-purpose flour

1¹/₄ teaspoons baking soda

³/₄ teaspoon salt

1 cup unsalted butter (2 sticks), slightly
    softened

1¹/₂ cups sugar

3 large eggs

2 teaspoons vanilla extract

4 cups White-Chocolate Cream-Cheese
    Frosting (recipe follows)

Food coloring

① MAKE THE BATTER: Preheat the oven to 350°F. Lightly butter two 8-inch cake pans. Line the bottoms with parchment paper and butter the paper. Set aside. Combine the boiling water and cocoa in a medium bowl. Stir in the buttermilk and set aside. Sift the flour, baking soda, and salt together into a medium bowl and set aside. Beat the butter in a large bowl with a mixer set on medium speed until light. Add the sugar and beat until light and fluffy—about 5 minutes. Add the eggs, one at a time, beating well after each addition. Add the vanilla and beat until the mixture is smooth and light. Reduce the mixer speed to low and add the flour mixture by thirds, alternating with the buttermilk mixture and ending with the dry ingredients, blending well after each addition until smooth.

② BAKE THE CAKE: Pour the batter into the prepared pans and spread evenly. Bake until a tester inserted into the center of each cake layer comes out clean—about 45 minutes. Cool in the cake pans on wire racks for 30 minutes. Use a knife to loosen the cake layers from the sides of the pans and invert the cake layers onto the wire racks. Peel off the parchment paper and cool completely.

③ FROST THE CAKE: Transfer 1 cup White-Chocolate Cream-Cheese Frosting to a small bowl, stir in the color of your choice, and set aside. Place a cake layer on a serving plate, top with 1 cup of remaining frosting and spread evenly. Top with the second cake layer. Cover the top and sides of the cake with a thin coating of frosting and chill for at least 1 hour. Spread the remaining frosting over the top and sides of the cake. Fill a pastry bag fitted with a decorating tip (such as a star or shell) with the colored frosting and decorate the cake as desired. Store, covered, in the refrigerator for up to 2 days. Let stand at room temperature for 15 minutes before serving.

(CONTINUED)

NUTRITION INFORMATION PER SERVING WITHOUT FROSTING—PROTEIN: 8.5 G; FAT: 42.5 G; CARBOHYDRATE: 83.5 G; FIBER: 3 G; SODIUM: 441 MG; CHOLESTEROL: 150 MG; CALORIES: 726.

④ TO MAKE THE CANOPY: Cut a 6- to 8-inch circle out of wrapping paper. Using scissors, make one cut from the edge of the circle to the center of the circle. Overlap the cut section slightly to create a pointed "dome" and glue or staple the overlapping edges together. Insert the candy sticks (straws are an alternative) 1 inch from the edge of the cake, evenly spaced around the cake, and insert 1 candy stick in the center. Decorate the base of the candy sticks and the cake with piping as desired. Set the canopy on top of the candy sticks.

White-Chocolate Cream-Cheese Frosting

10 ounces white chocolate, chopped

10 ounces cream cheese, softened

10 tablespoons unsalted butter (1¼ sticks), softened

1¼ teaspoons vanilla extract

¼ teaspoon salt

2½ cups confectioners' sugar

MAKE THE FROSTING: Melt the chocolate in a bowl set over a pot of gently simmering water. Remove from the heat, cool until lukewarm, and set aside. Combine the cream cheese and butter in a large bowl and beat with a mixer set on medium speed until smooth. Add the melted chocolate, vanilla, and salt and mix until incorporated. Add the confectioners' sugar and beat until the frosting is light and fluffy. Store refrigerated in an airtight container for up to 2 days.

NUTRITION INFORMATION PER ¼-CUP SERVING OF FROSTING—PROTEIN: .2 G; FAT: 15.4 G; CARBOHYDRATE: 18.8 G; FIBER: 0 G; SODIUM: 3.5 MG; CHOLESTEROL: 41.8 MG; CALORIES: 211.

Fresh Fig Cake

Not your standard fruit cake, this versatile fig version can be served year-round—all day long—for a sweet breakfast treat or the perfect finish to a meal. Serve warm right from the oven so the cinnamon flavor is at its most intense. ✳ MAKES 8 SERVINGS (ONE 9-INCH CAKE)

1 cup all-purpose flour

1 teaspoon baking powder

1/2 teaspoon ground cinnamon

1/4 cup butter (1/2 stick), softened

2/3 cup sugar

1/4 cup vanilla nonfat yogurt

2 large eggs

12 large fresh purple figs, stemmed and
   cut lengthwise in half

① MAKE THE BATTER: Preheat the oven to 350°F. Lightly coat a 9-inch springform pan with butter or vegetable-oil nonstick cooking spray. Set aside. Combine the flour, baking powder, and cinnamon in a small bowl and set aside. Beat the butter and sugar in a large bowl with a mixer set on medium speed until well mixed. Beat in the yogurt and eggs until blended. Reduce the mixer speed to low and beat in the flour mixture by thirds, beating until the batter is smooth.

② BAKE THE CAKE: Pour the batter into the prepared pan and spread evenly. Arrange the figs, alternating cut sides and skin sides up, around the rim of the pan on top of the batter. Arrange the remaining figs in the center.

③ Bake until a tester inserted into the cake near the center comes out clean— about 40 minutes. Cool in the pan on a wire rack to lukewarm. Use a knife to loosen the cake from the sides of the pan and remove the pan rim. Place the cake on a serving plate and serve warm.

NUTRITION INFORMATION PER SERVING—PROTEIN: 4 G; FAT: 7 G; CARBOHYDRATE: 48 G;
FIBER: 4 G; SODIUM: 118 MG; CHOLESTEROL: 69 MG; CALORIES: 268.

Gingerbread Stack Cake

This spicy, fragrant gingerbread is bursting with the flavor and aroma of ginger. Layered with swirls of mascarpone and garnished with a sprinkle of confettilike lemon zest, this tender three-layer cake will make a statement on any buffet table. Accentuate its height even more by placing it on a cake stand. ✳ MAKES 24 SERVINGS (ONE 8-INCH 3-LAYER CAKE)

5 cups all-purpose flour

5 teaspoons ground ginger

4 teaspoons baking soda

2 teaspoons ground cinnamon

1 teaspoon ground allspice

1 teaspoon ground nutmeg

1 teaspoon salt

1 cup unsalted butter (2 sticks), softened

1 cup firmly packed light brown sugar

4 large eggs

3 tablespoons grated lemon zest

2 cups boiling water

1 1/2 cups dark molasses

3/4 cup fresh lemon juice

3 cups mascarpone cheese

1/4 cup plus 2 tablespoons granulated sugar

1/4 cup heavy cream

Candied lemon peel (optional)

① MAKE THE BATTER: Preheat the oven to 350°F. Lightly coat three 8-inch cake pans with vegetable-oil cooking spray and set aside. Combine the flour, ginger, baking soda, cinnamon, allspice, nutmeg, and salt in a large mixing bowl and set aside. Beat the butter in a large bowl using a mixer set on medium-high speed for 3 minutes. Add the brown sugar and continue to beat until light and fluffy—about 3 more minutes. Reduce the speed to low and add the eggs, one at a time, beating well after each addition. Add 1 tablespoon of the lemon zest. Combine the boiling water, molasses, and 1/4 cup of the lemon juice in a medium bowl. Reduce the mixer speed to low and add the flour mixture by thirds, alternating with the molasses mixture and ending with the dry ingredients, until the batter is smooth.

② BAKE THE CAKE: Divide the batter equally among the prepared pans and spread evenly. Bake until a tester inserted into the center of each cake layer comes out clean—20 to 25 minutes. Cool in the pans on wire racks for 5 minutes. Use a knife to loosen the cake layers from the sides of the pans and invert the layers onto the wire racks to cool completely.

③ ASSEMBLE THE CAKE: Combine the mascarpone, remaining lemon zest, lemon juice, sugar, and heavy cream in a large bowl and gently beat until well blended. Place a cake layer on a serving plate and spread one third of the mascarpone filling over the top. Repeat with the remaining 2 layers and filling. Garnish with candied lemon peel, if desired. Store refrigerated for up to 2 days.

NUTRITION INFORMATION PER SERVING—PROTEIN: 6.8 G; FAT: 37 G; CARBOHYDRATE: 51.7 G; FIBER: 1.2 G; SODIUM: 386 MG; CHOLESTEROL: 237 MG; CALORIES: 552.

Peppermint Cake

Fresh peppermint leaves are the refreshing surprise in this sweet dessert of moist marbled angel cake wrapped in creamy white-chocolate frosting. Delicate fresh pansies and mint leaves are all that's needed for garnish. In farmers' markets, peppermint is also sometimes called black mint—you'll know it by its bold fragrance. ✳ MAKES 12 SERVINGS (ONE 10-INCH TUBE CAKE)

1 1/2 cups confectioners' sugar

1 cup all-purpose flour

1 1/2 cups egg whites (10 to 12 large eggs),
   at room temperature

1 1/2 teaspoons cream of tartar

1/4 teaspoon salt

3/4 cup granulated sugar

1 1/2 teaspoons vanilla extract

1 cup fresh peppermint leaves, finely
   chopped

1 teaspoon mint extract

6 drops green food coloring

White-Chocolate Frosting (recipe follows)

Pesticide-free pansies (optional)

① MAKE THE BATTER: Preheat the oven to 375°F. Sift the confectioners' sugar and flour into a medium-size bowl. Beat the egg whites, cream of tartar, and salt in a large bowl with a mixer set on high speed until foamy. Gradually beat in the granulated sugar until stiff, glossy peaks form. Beat in the vanilla. Sift the flour mixture over the beaten egg whites one fourth at a time, gently folding in the mixture with a rubber spatula or whisk until smooth.

② BAKE THE CAKE: Spoon half of the batter into a medium bowl and fold in the mint leaves, mint extract, and food coloring until blended. Spoon the plain and mint batters alternately into an ungreased 10- by 4-inch tube pan. With a small metal spatula, cut through the batter once to remove any large air bubbles. Bake until the center springs back when lightly touched—about 35 minutes. Invert the pan onto its legs and let the cake stand until completely cool. Use a thin knife to loosen the cake from the pan sides and center tube and invert onto a serving plate.

③ FROST THE CAKE: Spread the White-Chocolate Frosting over the top and sides of the cake. Garnish with pansies, if desired. To slice this tender cake, use a specially designed angel food cake cutter or 2 forks placed back-to-back and inserted from above to pull the cake apart into wedges. Store refrigerated for up to 3 days.

White-Chocolate Frosting

1 8-ounce package cream cheese, softened

1 6-ounce package white-chocolate
   squares, melted and cooled

1/2 cup unsalted butter (1 stick), cut into
   pieces and softened

1 tablespoon vanilla extract

Beat the cream cheese in a large bowl with a mixer set on medium speed until smooth. Gradually add the melted white chocolate, butter, and vanilla, beating until the frosting is smooth.

NUTRITION INFORMATION PER SERVING—PROTEIN: 6 G; FAT: 19 G; CARBOHYDRATE: 41 G; FIBER: 2 G; SODIUM: 152 MG; CHOLESTEROL: 46 MG; CALORIES: 358.

Spice Pound Cake

This tried-and-true pound cake takes on an autumn twist with the addition of brown sugar and nutmeg. Dust with confectioners' sugar for breakfast or serve spiked with fruit syrup for a tempting dessert. ✳ MAKES 14 SERVINGS (ONE 10-INCH BUNDT CAKE)

3 cups sifted cake flour

³/₄ teaspoon ground nutmeg

¹/₂ teaspoon salt

¹/₄ teaspoon baking power

¹/₄ teaspoon baking soda

1 cup butter (2 sticks), softened

2 cups granulated sugar

1 cup firmly packed light brown sugar

6 large eggs

1 cup sour cream

Confectioners' sugar (optional)

① MAKE THE BATTER: Preheat the oven to 325°F. Grease a 12-cup Bundt pan. Dust with flour and tap out the excess. Set aside. Combine the flour, nutmeg, salt, baking powder, and baking soda in a medium bowl. Set aside. Beat the butter and sugars in a large bowl with a mixer set on medium speed until light and fluffy—about 5 minutes. Beat in the eggs, one at a time, beating well after each addition. Reduce the mixer speed to low and add the flour mixture by thirds, alternating with the sour cream and ending with the dry ingredients, mixing just until the batter is smooth.

② BAKE THE CAKE: Pour the batter into the prepared pan and spread evenly. Bake until a tester inserted into the center of the cake comes out clean—about 1 hour 20 minutes. Cool in the pan on a wire rack for 10 minutes. Use a knife to loosen the cake from the side of the pan and invert onto a wire rack to cool completely. Sprinkle the cake with confectioners' sugar, if desired.

NUTRITION INFORMATION PER SERVING—PROTEIN: 6 G; FAT: 20 G; CARBOHYDRATE: 77 G; FIBER: 3 G; SODIUM: 259 MG; CHOLESTEROL: 132 MG; CALORIES: 499.

The Kitchen's Hummingbird Cake

Hummingbird cake is a banana-pineapple creation that has been enjoyed throughout the South since the mid-nineteenth century. This especially delicious—and classic—version comes from The Kitchen restaurant in Jeffersonville, New York. ✳ MAKES 12 SERVINGS (ONE 9-INCH 2-LAYER CAKE)

1 8-ounce can crushed pineapple in unsweetened juice

3 cups all-purpose flour

1 teaspoon baking soda

1 teaspoon ground cinnamon

1 teaspoon salt

2 cups sugar

1 1/4 cups vegetable oil

3 large eggs

2 cups very ripe mashed banana (about 5 bananas)

1 1/2 teaspoons vanilla extract

1 1/2 cups chopped toasted pecans

Cream-Cheese Frosting (recipe follows)

① MAKE THE BATTER: Preheat the oven to 350°F. Lightly butter two 9-inch cake pans. Line the bottoms with parchment paper and butter the paper. Set aside. Drain the pineapple, reserve 1/4 cup juice, and set aside. Sift the flour, baking soda, cinnamon, and salt together into a large bowl and set aside. Beat the sugar and oil in another large bowl using a mixer set on medium speed until smooth—about 3 minutes. Add the eggs, one at a time, beating after each addition until very light—about 2 minutes. Reduce the mixer speed to low, add the bananas, pineapple, the reserved juice, and vanilla and mix until just combined. Add the flour mixture by thirds, beating after each addition until smooth. Stir in 1/2 cup of the pecans.

② BAKE THE CAKE: Divide the batter equally between the prepared pans and bake until a tester inserted into the center of each cake layer comes out clean—about 45 minutes. Cool in the pans on wire racks for 20 minutes. Use a knife to loosen the cake layers from the sides of the pans and invert the cake layers onto the wire racks. Peel off the parchment paper. Cool completely.

③ FROST THE CAKE: Use a serrated knife to level the tops of the cake layers. Line the edge of a serving plate with 3-inch-wide strips of waxed or parchment paper and place a cake layer, trimmed side down, on top. Place 3/4 cup of the Cream-Cheese Frosting on top of the layer and spread evenly. Place the second cake layer, trimmed side down, on top of the first and cover the top and sides of the cake with the remaining icing. Sprinkle with the remaining pecans and serve. Store refrigerated for up to 4 days.

Cream-Cheese Frosting

12 ounces cream cheese, cut into pieces and slightly softened

1/2 cup unsalted butter (1 stick), cut into pieces and slightly softened

1 1/2 teaspoons vanilla extract

5 cups sifted confectioners' sugar

MAKE THE FROSTING: Combine the cream cheese and butter in a medium bowl. Using a mixer set on medium speed, beat until smooth—about 3 minutes. Add the vanilla. Gradually beat in the confectioners' sugar until well incorporated.

NUTRITION INFORMATION PER SERVING—PROTEIN: 8.5 G; FAT: 52 G; CARBOHYDRATE: 119 G; FIBER: 2.4 G; SODIUM: 385 MG; CHOLESTEROL: 105 MG; CALORIES: 957.

Banana-Caramel Cake

Fancier than the classic snack cake version, this layered rendition is not only swathed in caramel icing but it's filled with it, too. This recipe is an exception to the rule that all ingredients should be fresh: Use overripe bananas for the most intense flavor possible. ✴ MAKES 12 SERVINGS (ONE 9-INCH 2-LAYER CAKE)

2¹/₂ cups cake flour

2¹/₂ teaspoons baking powder

¹/₂ teaspoon baking soda

¹/₂ teaspoon salt

¹/₂ cup unsalted butter (1 stick), softened

1¹/₄ cups granulated sugar

2 large eggs

1¹/₂ teaspoons vanilla extract

¹/₂ cup buttermilk

1 cup mashed very ripe bananas
    (about 2 bananas)

Caramel Icing (recipe follows)

① MAKE THE BATTER: Preheat the oven to 350°F. Lightly coat two 9-inch cake pans with butter or vegetable-oil cooking spray. Dust with flour and tap out any excess. Set aside. Sift the flour, baking powder, baking soda, and salt together onto a large sheet of waxed or parchment paper. Resift the flour mixture into a medium bowl and set aside. Beat the butter in a large bowl using a mixer set on medium-high speed until light—about 1 minute. Add the sugar and continue to beat for 2 more minutes. Add the eggs, one at a time, beating well after each addition. Mix in the vanilla. Reduce the mixer speed to low and add the flour mixture by thirds, alternating with the buttermilk and bananas and ending with the dry ingredients. Mix just enough to blend the batter after each addition.

② BAKE THE CAKE: Divide the batter equally between the prepared pans and bake until a tester inserted into the center of each cake layer comes out clean—25 to 30 minutes. Cool in the cake pans on wire racks for 15 minutes. Use a knife to loosen the cake layers from the sides of the pans and invert the cake layers onto the wire rack to cool completely.

③ ICE THE CAKE: Use a serrated knife to level the tops of the cake layers, if necessary. Line the edges of a cake plate with 3-inch-wide strips of waxed or parchment paper and place a cake layer, trimmed side down, on top. Place 1 cup of the Caramel Icing on top of the layer and spread evenly. Place the second layer, trimmed side down on top and spread the remaining icing over the top and sides. Remove the paper strips and serve. Store refrigerated for up to 2 days.

(CONTINUED)

NUTRITION INFORMATION PER SERVING—PROTEIN: 3.5 G; FAT: 23.8 G; CARBOHYDRATE: 77.8 G; FIBER: .7 G; SODIUM: 291 MG; CHOLESTEROL: 74.8 MG; CALORIES: 528

Caramel Icing

3 cups firmly packed light brown sugar

1 1/2 cups heavy cream

1/2 teaspoon fresh lemon juice

5 tablespoons cold butter, cut into pieces

MAKE THE ICING: Combine the brown sugar, heavy cream, and lemon juice in a medium saucepan. Cook the mixture, without stirring, over medium-high heat until the mixture reaches the soft-ball stage (238°F) on a candy thermometer. Remove from the heat and cool the caramel mixture to 140°F. Place the butter on top of the cooled caramel mixture and remove the thermometer. Beat the caramel using a handheld mixer set on medium-high speed until it thickens enough to hold its shape, lightens in color, and changes from translucent to opaque—about 5 minutes. Use the icing immediately.

✳ Cool Caramel ✳

It's never a good idea to make any form of caramel—except caramel sauce—in humid weather or it will be sticky. Have your candy thermometer nearby while preparing caramel icing. Be careful not to overheat the sugar—the hotter the caramel, the harder it gets as it cools, making it more difficult to ice and slice a cake.

Skillet Cake with Carmelized Pears

The beauty of upside-down cakes is the pattern the fruit makes in the batter.
Maple syrup is a flavorful accent in this tender butter cake, which makes it especially delectable.

✳ MAKES 8 SERVINGS (ONE 10-INCH CAKE)

11 tablespoons butter (1 stick plus
    3 tablespoons), softened

³/₄ cup pure maple syrup, preferably
    grade AA

¹/₄ cup firmly packed light brown sugar

4 pears, peeled, cored, and cut
    lengthwise into thin slices

2 large egg yolks

1 large egg

¹/₂ cup sour cream

1 teaspoon vanilla extract

2 cups plus 2 tablespoons cake flour

¹/₄ cup granulated sugar

1 teaspoon baking powder

¹/₄ teaspoon baking soda

¹/₄ teaspoon salt

① ARRANGE THE FRUIT: Preheat the oven to 350°F. Melt the 3 tablespoons butter in a 10-inch cast-iron skillet over medium-high heat. Stir in ¼ cup of the maple syrup and the brown sugar. Stir until the sugar dissolves. Bring to a boil and cook for 2 minutes. Remove from the heat and arrange the pear slices in the skillet in a circle, overlapping the slices, with the wider ends facing out. Set aside.

② MAKE THE BATTER: Whisk the egg yolks, egg, ¼ cup sour cream, remaining maple syrup, and vanilla together in a small bowl. Set aside. Combine the flour, granulated sugar, baking powder, baking soda, and salt in a large bowl. With a mixer set on medium speed, blend in the remaining butter and remaining sour cream. Beat in the egg mixture in three additions, scraping down the sides of the bowl after each addition.

③ BAKE THE CAKE: Pour the batter over the pears in the skillet and spread evenly. Bake until a tester inserted into the center of the cake comes out clean—50 to 60 minutes. Cool in the pan on a wire rack for 5 minutes. Invert onto a cake plate and serve warm or at room temperature. Store at room temperature for up to 2 days.

NUTRITION INFORMATION PER SERVING—PROTEIN: 5 G; FAT: 21 G; CARBOHYDRATE: 66 G;
FIBER: 3 G; SODIUM: 293 MG; CHOLESTEROL: 127 MG; CALORIES: 469.

Fresh Strawberry Cake

Nothing signals summer's arrival more than the combination of fresh strawberries, whipped cream, and cake. If you don't have time to make the cake from scratch, speed up the process by using a white cake mix, adding 1/8 teaspoon red food coloring, and reducing the liquid in the mix by 1/3 cup. Use store-bought whipped cream to save even more time. ✱ MAKES 10 SERVINGS (TWO 9-INCH CAKES)

2 1/2 cups cake flour

1 1/4 teaspoons baking powder

3/4 teaspoon salt

1/2 teaspoon baking soda

3/4 cup butter (1 1/2 sticks), softened

1 1/2 cups plus 2 tablespoons sugar

1 cup strawberry preserves

4 large eggs

3/4 teaspoon vanilla extract

1/8 teaspoon red food coloring

1/2 cup buttermilk

1 3/4 cups heavy cream

1 1/2 pints fresh strawberries, hulled

✱ Easy Homemade ✱ Preserves

For a quick batch of fresh strawberry preserves: Cook 2 pounds hulled strawberries and 4 cups sugar for about 1 hour over medium-low heat to a thick syrup consistency.

① MAKE THE BATTER: Preheat the oven to 350°F. Lightly butter two 9-inch cake pans and line with parchment paper. Lightly coat the paper and pan sides with butter, dust with flour, and tap out the excess. Set aside. Sift the flour, baking powder, salt, and baking soda together into a medium bowl and set aside. Beat the butter and the 1 1/2 cups sugar in a large bowl using a mixer set on medium-high speed until light and fluffy—about 5 minutes. Add 3/4 cup of the preserves and the eggs, one at a time, beating well after each addition. Scrape down the sides of the bowl and beat in the vanilla and food coloring. Reduce the mixer speed to low and add the flour mixture by thirds, alternating with the buttermilk and ending with the dry ingredients, mixing just until the batter is smooth.

② BAKE THE CAKE: Divide the batter equally between the prepared pans and spread evenly. Bake until a tester inserted in the center of each cake layer comes out clean—20 to 30 minutes. Cool in the cake pans on wire racks for 10 minutes. Use a knife to loosen the cake layers from the sides of the pans and invert onto the wire racks. Peel off the parchment paper and cool completely.

③ ASSEMBLE THE CAKE: Place one cake layer on a serving plate and set aside. Beat the cream and remaining sugar in a large bowl using a mixer set on medium speed until soft peaks form. Spread over the top of the layer. (Wrap and freeze the remaining layer for up to 2 months.) Top with the strawberries and drizzle with the remaining preserves. Serve immediately.

NUTRITION INFORMATION PER SERVING—PROTEIN: 6.9 G; FAT: 31.5 G; CARBOHYDRATE: 84.4 G; FIBER: 1.2 G; SODIUM: 358 MG; CHOLESTEROL: 178.3 MG; CALORIES: 639.

Burnt-Sugar Pound Cake

The deep brown-colored sugar syrup adds complex sweetness to this buttery pound cake.
Serve as is or drizzle the burnt-sugar syrup over rich vanilla ice cream atop each slice.

* MAKES 12 SERVINGS (ONE 9- BY 5-INCH CAKE)

2²/₃ cups sugar

3 teaspoons fresh lemon juice

2 teaspoons vanilla extract

2 cups all-purpose flour

1/2 teaspoon salt

1 cup unsalted butter (2 sticks), softened

1 vanilla bean, split lengthwise and seeds
    scraped

5 large eggs

* Vanilla *

Always use pure vanilla extract rather than synthetic varieties. The label on the bottle will indicate if the extract is naturally made. Store vanilla extract and vanilla beans in a cool, dark place—do not refrigerate. Before storing, wrap beans in plastic and place inside an airtight container to retain moisture.

① MAKE THE BURNT-SUGAR SYRUP: Preheat the oven to 325°F. Butter a 9- by 5- by 3-inch loaf pan. Dust with flour and tap out the excess. Set aside. Bring a small pot of water to a simmer and maintain the simmer. Combine 1⅓ cups sugar and 1 teaspoon lemon juice in a small nonstick saucepan over medium heat and cook until the sugar along the edges of the pan begins to bubble. Remove from the heat and stir until liquefied and dark amber—about 2 minutes. Let stand for 1 minute. Slowly add 1 cup simmering water. The mixture will steam and thicken. Place the saucepan over low heat and cook, stirring occasionally until the sugar syrup is smooth—about 15 minutes. Carefully measure out ¼ cup of the syrup and set aside. Add 1 teaspoon of the vanilla and the remaining lemon juice to the remaining syrup and keep warm.

② MAKE THE BATTER: Sift the flour and salt together into a medium bowl. Beat the butter, remaining sugar, and vanilla bean seeds in a large bowl using a mixer set on high speed until light and fluffy—about 5 minutes. Add the eggs, one at a time, beating well after each addition. Add the reserved ¼ cup burnt-sugar syrup, remaining vanilla, and flour, in fourths, beating well after each addition.

③ BAKE THE CAKE: Pour the batter into the prepared pan and spread evenly. Bake until a tester inserted into the center of the cake comes out clean—about 1 hour. Cool in the pan on a wire rack for 5 minutes. Use a knife to loosen the cake from the sides of the pan and invert onto the wire rack. Invert the cake, right side up, and brush the warm cake with ½ cup burnt-sugar syrup. Serve at room temperature with the remaining syrup alongside. Store at room temperature for up to 3 days.

NUTRITION INFORMATION PER SERVING—PROTEIN: 4.9 G; FAT: 17.6 G; CARBOHYDRATE: 60.7 G; FIBER: 0.7 G; SODIUM: 118 MG; CHOLESTEROL: 130 MG; CALORIES: 417.

Toasted Coconut Coffee Cake

This scrumptious coffee cake, which is delicious for breakfast or brunch, can be made the day before you plan to serve it. Cover it with foil and reheat it in a low oven to bring out all the heavenly toasted coconut flavor and aroma. ✳ MAKES 12 SERVINGS (ONE 9-INCH CAKE)

COFFEE-CAKE TOPPING:

1 1/2 cups sweetened flaked coconut

1/2 cup all-purpose flour

1/2 cup firmly packed light brown sugar

1 1/2 tablespoons ground cinnamon

6 tablespoons unsalted butter, melted

CAKE:

1 3/4 cups all-purpose flour

1 teaspoon baking powder

1/2 teaspoon salt

5 large egg yolks

1/3 cup granulated sugar

1/4 cup firmly packed light brown sugar

1 1/2 teaspoons vanilla extract

3/4 cup unsalted butter (1 1/2 sticks), softened

1/2 cup sour cream

① MAKE THE COFFEE-CAKE TOPPING: Combine the coconut, flour, brown sugar, and cinnamon in a small bowl. Add the melted butter and toss until evenly moistened. Set aside.

② MAKE THE BATTER: Preheat the oven to 325°F. Lightly butter a 9-inch springform pan and set aside. Combine the flour, baking powder, and salt in a medium bowl and set aside. Beat the egg yolks, sugars, and vanilla using a mixer set on high speed until the mixture is thick and pale yellow—about 2 minutes. Beat in the softened butter and sour cream until blended. Reduce the mixer speed to low and add the flour mixture by thirds, beating just until smooth.

③ BAKE THE CAKE: Pour the batter into the prepared pan, spread evenly, and sprinkle with the topping. Bake until a tester inserted into the center of the cake comes out clean—55 to 60 minutes. Cool in the pan on a wire rack for 1 hour. Remove the rim of the pan. Serve warm.

NUTRITION INFORMATION PER SERVING—PROTEIN: 4.4 G; FAT: 24.6 G; CARBOHYDRATE: 37.9 G; FIBER: 1.6 G; SODIUM: 159 MG; CHOLESTEROL: 140 MG; CALORIES: 386.

Red Velvet Cake

This four-layer cake has been enjoyed for more than a half century. It was originally served at New York City's Waldorf-Astoria hotel and has remained a classic ever since. You can prepare the layers a day in advance and then assemble the cake the next day, if you like. ✳ MAKES 12 SERVINGS (ONE 9-INCH 4-LAYER CAKE)

1/2 cup unsalted butter (1 stick), softened

1 1/2 cups sugar

4 large egg yolks

1/4 cup unsweetened cocoa

3 tablespoons red food coloring

1 1/2 teaspoons vanilla extract

1 cup buttermilk

1 teaspoon salt

2 1/4 cups sifted cake flour

1 teaspoon baking soda

1 teaspoon white vinegar

Cooked Vanilla Icing (recipe follows)

① MAKE THE BATTER: Preheat the oven to 350°F. Lightly coat two 9-inch cake pans with butter or vegetable-oil cooking spray. Dust with flour and tap out any excess. Set aside. Beat the butter and sugar in a large bowl using a mixer set on medium-high speed until light and fluffy—about 5 minutes. Add the egg yolks and continue to beat for 1 more minute. Stir the cocoa, food coloring, and vanilla together in a small bowl. Reduce the mixer speed to low and beat in the cocoa mixture. Combine the buttermilk and salt in a glass measuring cup. Add the flour by thirds, alternating with the buttermilk mixture and ending with the dry ingredients. Mix the baking soda and vinegar together in a cup and blend into the batter, beating until smooth.

② BAKE THE CAKE: Divide the batter equally between the prepared pans and spread evenly. Bake until a tester inserted into the center of each cake layer comes out clean—about 30 minutes. Cool in the pans on wire racks for 15 minutes. Use a knife to loosen the cake layers from the sides of the pans and invert the layers onto the wire racks to cool completely.

③ ICE THE CAKE: Use a serrated knife to split each layer into 2 even layers. Line the edges of a cake plate with 3-inch-wide strips of waxed or parchment paper and place a cake layer, cut side down, on top. Place 1 cup of the Cooked Vanilla Icing on top of the layer and spread evenly. Repeat with 2 more layers. Top with the fourth layer and cover the top and sides of the cake with the remaining icing. Store refrigerated for up to 4 days.

Cooked Vanilla Icing

2 cups milk

1/4 cup plus 2 teaspoons all-purpose flour

2 cups unsalted butter (4 sticks), softened

2 cups confectioners' sugar

2 teaspoons vanilla extract

MAKE THE ICING: Whisk the milk and flour together in a medium sauce-pan until smooth. Set the saucepan over medium heat and cook, stirring constantly, until thickened—about 5 minutes. Remove from the heat, cool to room temperature, and set aside. Beat the butter and confectioners' sugar in a medium bowl using a mixer set on high speed until light. Add the vanilla and reduce the mixer speed to medium. Slowly add the cooled milk mixture and beat for 1 more minute.

NUTRITION INFORMATION PER SERVING OF CAKE—PROTEIN: 5.5 G; FAT: 4.2 G; CARBOHYDRATE: 65.6 G; FIBER: 1 G; SODIUM: 333 MG; CHOLESTEROL: 181 MG; CALORIES: 651.

The Kitchen's Chambord Layer Cake

Rich fruit preserves separate the three layers of The Kitchen restaurant's Chambord Layer Cake, while a black-raspberry–flavored buttercream imparts a pale pink hue.

✳ MAKES 12 SERVINGS (ONE 9-INCH 3-LAYER CAKE)

1½ cups self-rising flour

1¼ cups all-purpose flour

1 cup milk

1 tablespoon vanilla extract

1 cup unsalted butter (2 sticks), softened

2 cups granulated sugar

4 large eggs

1 cup black cherry preserves

Black Raspberry Buttercream
   (recipe follows)

① MAKE THE BATTER: Preheat the oven to 350°F. Lightly butter three 9-inch cake pans. Line the bottoms with parchment paper and butter the paper. Set aside. Combine the flours in a medium bowl and set aside. Combine the milk and vanilla in a glass measuring cup and set aside. Beat the butter in a large bowl using a mixer set on medium speed until smooth—about 3 minutes. Gradually add the sugar and beat until light and fluffy—about 3 more minutes. Add the eggs, one at a time, beating well after each addition. Reduce the mixer speed to low and add the flour mixture in 2 additions, alternating with the milk mixture and ending with the dry ingredients, mixing after each addition until the batter is smooth.

② BAKE THE CAKE: Evenly divide the batter among the prepared pans and bake until a tester inserted into the center of each cake layer comes out clean—about 30 minutes. Cool in the pans on wire racks for 10 minutes. Use a knife to loosen the cake layers from the sides of the pans and invert the cake layers onto the wire racks. Peel off the parchment paper and cool completely.

③ ASSEMBLE THE CAKE: Line the edges of a serving plate with 3-inch-wide strips of waxed or parchment paper and place a cake layer on top. Place ½ cup of the preserves on top of the layer and spread evenly. Top with the second layer and the remaining preserves. Place the third layer on top and cover the top and sides of the cake with the frosting.

Black Raspberry Buttercream

1 cup unsalted butter (2 sticks), softened

1 tablespoon heavy cream

1 tablespoon Chambord

1 tablespoon cranberry juice

4 cups sifted confectioners' sugar

MAKE THE FROSTING: Beat the butter in a medium bowl using a mixer set on medium speed until smooth—about 3 minutes. Add the heavy cream, liqueur, and cranberry juice and beat until smooth. Gradually add the confectioners' sugar, beating until smooth

NUTRITION INFORMATION PER SERVING—PROTEIN: 6.5 G; FAT: 40.7 G; CARBOHYDRATE: 115 G; FIBER: .8 G; SODIUM: 245 MG; CHOLESTEROL: 184 MG; CALORIES: 869.

Rich Chocolate Layer Cake

Adapted from Hellmann's Super-Moist Chocolate Mayo Cake recipe,
this cake is particularly moist, thanks to a surprise ingredient: mayonnaise.

* MAKES 14 SERVINGS (ONE 8-INCH 4-LAYER CAKE)

1 box devil's food cake mix

1/4 cup unsweetened cocoa

1 cup mayonnaise

3 large eggs

1 cup water

2 16-ounce containers chocolate frosting

1/4 cup sour cream

2 teaspoons vanilla extract

1 cup sweetened flaked coconut, toasted

1/2 cup chopped almonds, toasted

① MAKE THE BATTER: Preheat the oven to 350°F. Lightly butter two 8-inch cake pans. Line the bottoms with parchment paper and butter the paper. Dust with flour and tap out any excess. Set aside. Beat the cake mix, cocoa, mayonnaise, eggs, and water in a large bowl with a mixer set on low speed until blended. Increase the mixer speed to high and beat for 2 more minutes.

② BAKE THE CAKE: Divide the batter equally between the prepared pans and spread evenly. Bake until a tester inserted into the center of each cake layer comes out clean—about 35 minutes. Cool in the cake pans on wire racks for 20 minutes. Use a knife to loosen the cake layers from the sides of the pans and invert the cake layers onto the wire racks. Peel off the parchment paper and cool completely.

③ MAKE THE FILLING: Whisk the frosting, sour cream, and vanilla together in a large bowl. Transfer 1½ cups of the frosting to a medium bowl and stir in the almonds and coconut. Set aside.

④ FROST THE CAKE: Using a serrated knife, split each cake layer in half and brush away any excess crumbs. Line the edges of a serving plate with 3-inch-wide strips of waxed or parchment paper and place a cake layer, split side down, on top. Place ⅓ of the filling on top of the layer and spread evenly. Place a second layer on top and cover with another ⅓ of the filling. Repeat with the third cake layer and remaining filling and top with the final cake layer. Spread the frosting over the top of the cake, smoothing out to the edges. Spread the remaining frosting around the sides. Serve or store covered for up to 4 days.

* Fancy Frosting *

To make swoops in the icing, use the back of a teaspoon or tablespoon, depending on the size of swoop required. The rounded tip of an inch-wide offset spatula will make large, dramatic swoops.

NUTRITION INFORMATION PER SERVING—PROTEIN: 4.8 G; FAT: 36.3 G; CARBOHYDRATE: 68.5 G; FIBER: 2.9 G; SODIUM: 579 MG; CHOLESTEROL: 56.8 MG; CALORIES: 618.

Coconut Cloud Cake

Whether fresh-shaved or flaked—coconut is the star of this elegant cake. Packaged flaked coconut has added sugar so it contributes extra sweetness, while fresh coconut meat offers a subtle nutty flavor to the cake. Use whichever you prefer (see box). Sprinkle the coconut on the top and sides of the cake while the frosting is still soft so that the airy pieces stay on. ✱ MAKES 12 SERVINGS (ONE 9-INCH 3-LAYER CAKE)

4 cups plus 2 tablespoons sifted cake flour

1 1/2 tablespoons baking powder

3/4 teaspoon salt

3/4 cup unsalted butter (1 1/2 sticks), softened

2 1/4 cups sugar

6 large egg whites, at room temperature

2 1/4 teaspoons vanilla extract

1 1/2 cups milk

Lemon Curd (recipe follows)

Fluffy Meringue Frosting (recipe follows)

3/4 cup sweetened flaked coconut or 1 6-inch-diameter fresh coconut

① MAKE THE BATTER: Preheat the oven to 350°F. Lightly coat three 9-inch cake pans with butter or vegetable-oil cooking spray. Dust with flour and tap out any excess. Set aside. Sift the flour, baking powder, and salt together in a medium bowl and set aside. Beat the butter and sugar in a separate large bowl using a mixer set on high speed, until well combined. Add the egg whites and vanilla and continue to beat until light and fluffy—about 2 more minutes. Reduce the mixer speed to low and add half the flour mixture. Beat just until the flour is no longer visible. Add the milk and beat for 1 minute. Add the remaining flour mixture and beat for 1 more minute.

② BAKE THE CAKE: Divide the batter equally among the cake pans and spread evenly. Bake until the tops of the cakes spring back when lightly touched and a tester inserted into the center of each cake layer comes out clean—30 to 35 minutes. Cool in the pans on wire racks for 15 minutes. Use a knife to loosen the cake layers from the sides of the pans and invert the layers onto the wire rack to cool completely.

③ FROST THE CAKE: Use a serrated knife to level the tops of the cake layers, if necessary. Line the edges of a cake plate with 3-inch-wide strips of waxed or parchment paper and place a cake layer, trimmed side down, on top. Place ¾ cup of the Lemon Curd on top of the layer and spread evenly. Place the second layer, trimmed side down, on top of the first and spread with ¾ cup Lemon Curd. Top with the third layer, trimmed side down, cover the top and sides of the cake with the Fluffy Meringue Frosting, and sprinkle all over with the coconut. Remove the paper strips and serve. Store at room temperature for up to 4 days.

(CONTINUED)

NUTRITION INFORMATION PER SERVING—PROTEIN: 7.9 G; FAT: 16.3 G; CARBOHYDRATE: 78.6 G; FIBER: 1.1 G; SODIUM: 321 MG; CHOLESTEROL: 132 MG; CALORIES: 487.

Lemon Curd

4 large egg yolks

3 large eggs

3/4 cup sugar

1/2 cup fresh lemon juice (about 3 lemons)

2 tablespoons milk

1 tablespoon cornstarch

6 tablespoons unsalted butter, cut into
    pieces

MAKE THE LEMON CURD: Use a whisk to lightly beat the egg yolks and eggs together in a medium nonreactive saucepan. Stir in the sugar, lemon juice, milk, and cornstarch. Add the butter and set the saucepan over medium-low heat. Cook, whisking constantly, being sure to reach all around the sides and corners of the pan, until the mixture thickens—5 to 8 minutes. Do not allow the curd to boil. The resulting curd should have the consistency of a light pudding. Remove from the heat and cool the Lemon Curd for 5 minutes. Strain the cooled curd through a fine sieve. Store refrigerated in an airtight container for up to 1 week.

Fluffy Meringue Frosting

1/2 cup light corn syrup

1/2 cup sugar

2 large egg whites

2 tablespoons water

1/8 teaspoon salt

1 1/2 teaspoons vanilla extract

MAKE THE MERINGUE: Combine the light corn syrup, sugar, egg whites, water, and salt in a double boiler set over barely simmering water. Using a handheld mixer set on high speed, beat until the mixture is light and fluffy— about 6 minutes. Remove from the heat and beat in the vanilla. Continue to beat until the meringue forms stiff peaks—about 1 more minute.

* Opening a Coconut *

To open a fresh coconut, preheat the oven to 350°F. Pierce two of the eyes at one end of a coconut with a screwdriver or ice pick. Drain the coconut water and reserve for another use. (Use within 24 hours or freeze.) Bake the coconut for 20 minutes. Let cool slightly. Tap lightly with a hammer to crack the shell and loosen the meat inside. Wrap the coconut in a clean towel and place on a sturdy, hard surface. Hit the coconut hard with the hammer to break it into pieces. Unwrap and pry the white meat from the hard shell. Use a paring knife to carefully peel away the brown skin from the coconut meat. Use a vegetable peeler to shave the coconut meat. Unused coconut meat may be frozen in an airtight container for up to 2 months.

Cranberry-Apple Upside-Down Cake

This jewel-toned cake is a showcase for some of the fall season's classic flavors.
Just a touch of honey makes the fruit topping glisten. Garnish the serving plate with lady apples
and cranberries for some seasonal color. * MAKES 12 SERVINGS (ONE 9-INCH CAKE)

CRANBERRY-APPLE TOPPING:

2 tablespoons butter, softened

1/3 cup sugar

2 tablespoons honey

2/3 cup fresh or frozen cranberries

2 Fuji or Granny Smith apples, peeled,
   cored, and thinly sliced

CAKE:

2 cups all-purpose flour

1/2 teaspoon ground cloves

3/4 teaspoon baking powder

1/2 teaspoon baking soda

1/2 teaspoon salt

1/2 cup butter (1 stick), softened

1 1/3 cups sugar

2 large eggs

1 teaspoon vanilla extract

2/3 cup buttermilk

Cranberries, lady apples, and fresh mint
   sprig (optional)

① PREPARE THE PAN: Preheat the oven to 350°F. Remove the rim from a 9-inch springform pan and place two 12-inch squares of waxed or parchment paper over the bottom of the pan. Carefully replace the rim, leaving the edges of the paper outside the pan. Smooth the edges up over the side of the pan. Generously coat the inside of the pan with vegetable-oil cooking spray.

② PREPARE THE CRANBERRY-APPLE TOPPING: Spread the butter over the bottom of the prepared pan and top with the sugar and honey. Arrange 3 tablespoons cranberries around the outer edge of the pan bottom. Arrange overlapping apple slices in a circle inside the cranberries, leaving a 2½-inch space in the center. Arrange the apple slices around the edge, forming a circle, and fill with the remaining cranberries.

③ MAKE THE BATTER: Combine the flour, cloves, baking powder, baking soda, and salt in a medium bowl. Set aside. Beat the butter and sugar in a large bowl with a mixer set on medium speed until light and fluffy. Beat in the eggs, one at a time, beating well after each addition, then beat in the vanilla. Reduce the mixer speed to low and add the flour mixture by thirds, alternating with the buttermilk and ending with the dry ingredients, until a smooth batter forms.

④ BAKE THE CAKE: Spoon the batter evenly over the Cranberry-Apple Topping. Place the springform pan in a shallow baking pan. Bake the cake until a tester inserted into the center of the cake comes out clean—60 to 75 minutes. (The top of the cake will appear quite brown because of the cloves— this does not indicate that it is baked through.) Cool in the pan on a wire rack for 5 minutes. Use a knife to loosen the cake from the pan sides. Place a serving plate, upside down, on top of the cake. Using pot holders and holding the serving plate and pan together tightly, carefully invert the cake. Remove the rim of the pan, then remove the pan bottom and peel off the waxed paper. Cool the cake until ready to serve. If not served within 2 or 3 hours, cover and refrigerate. Set out at room temperature for 30 minutes before serving. If desired, garnish plate with cranberries, lady apple, and mint.

NUTRITION INFORMATION PER SERVING WITHOUT CRANBERRIES, LADY APPLE, OR MINT—PROTEIN: 4 G; FAT: 11 G; CARBOHYDRATE: 53 G; FIBER: 2 G; SODIUM: 265 MG; CHOLESTEROL: 62 MG; CALORIES: 320.

Pistachio Semolina Honey Cake

The combination of semolina (coarse-ground durum wheat) and a richly flavored honey syrup gives this cake its enticing texture. Honey, used here in place of other sweeteners, adds a unique layer of flavor while contributing moistness to this dense cake. * MAKES 10 SERVINGS (ONE 10-INCH CAKE)

CAKE:

³/₄ cup all-purpose flour

³/₄ cup semolina

1¹/₂ teaspoons baking powder

¹/₂ teaspoon salt

4 large eggs

²/₃ cup sugar

¹/₂ cup vegetable oil

1 cup finely ground pistachios

1 teaspoon grated lemon zest

SYRUP:

1 cup plus 2 tablespoons honey

1 cup water

1 tablespoon fresh lemon juice

1 1-inch piece honeycomb (optional)

2 tablespoons chopped pistachios (optional)

---

* Sticky Situation *

Avoid a sticky spoon or measuring cup when using honey: Lightly coat the spoon or cup with oil or vegetable-oil cooking spray and the honey will slide out!

---

① MAKE THE BATTER: Preheat the oven to 350°F. Lightly coat a 10-inch springform pan with vegetable-oil cooking spray. Combine the flour, semolina, baking powder, and salt in a medium bowl. Set aside. Beat the eggs and sugar in a large bowl with a mixer set on high speed until thick and pale—about 5 minutes. Reduce the mixer speed to low and slowly add the oil, beating until blended. With a whisk stir in the flour mixture until combined. Stir the pistachios and lemon zest into the batter.

② BAKE THE CAKE: Pour the batter into the prepared pan and spread evenly. Bake until golden and a tester inserted into the center of the cake comes out clean—30 to 35 minutes.

③ PREPARE THE SYRUP: Meanwhile, combine 1 cup of the honey, water, and lemon juice in a 1-quart saucepan and bring to a boil over high heat. Boil until reduced by half—about 10 minutes. Cool to room temperature.

④ SOAK THE CAKE: Using a toothpick or skewer, poke deep holes into the hot cake in the pan. Drizzle half of the syrup evenly over the top of the cake, allowing it to be absorbed before drizzling the remaining syrup over the cake. Cool the cake completely. Remove the rim of the pan. Carefully transfer the cake to a cake plate. Drizzle the remaining 2 tablespoons honey over the top of the cake. Garnish with the honeycomb and pistachio nuts, if desired. Store at room temperature for up to 3 days.

NUTRITION INFORMATION PER SERVING—PROTEIN: 7 G; FAT: 21 G; CARBOHYDRATE: 65 G; FIBER: 2.5 G; SODIUM: 303 MG; CHOLESTEROL: 85 MG; CALORIES: 460.

Café au Lait Chocolate Cake

The name of this cake inevitably conjures up visions of sitting at a bistro on the Left Bank in Paris. Cocoa, coffee, and vanilla add up to a very rich batter, but the luscious coffee buttercream topping is literally the frosting on the cake. ✱ MAKES 16 SERVINGS (ONE 9-INCH 4-LAYER CAKE)

¹/₂ cup Dutch-processed unsweetened cocoa

1 cup hot strong coffee

2¹/₄ cups sifted cake flour

1¹/₂ cups sugar

1 tablespoon baking powder

¹/₂ teaspoon salt

³/₄ cup unsalted butter (1¹/₂ sticks), softened

3 large eggs

2 teaspoons vanilla extract

Coffee Buttercream (recipe follows)

① MAKE THE BATTER: Preheat the oven to 350°F. Lightly butter two 9-inch cake pans. Line the bottoms with parchment paper and butter the paper. Flour the pans and tap out any excess. Set aside. Whisk the cocoa and coffee together in a small bowl until smooth and set aside to cool. Combine the flour, sugar, baking powder, and salt in a large bowl. Add the butter and cocoa mixture and beat with a mixer set on low speed. Increase the speed to high and continue beating for 2 more minutes. Whisk the eggs and vanilla together in a small bowl and gradually add to the flour mixture. Continue to beat, scraping down the sides of the bowl two or three times, until combined.

② BAKE THE CAKE: Divide the batter equally between the prepared pans and spread evenly. Bake until golden brown and a tester inserted into the center of each cake layer comes out clean—25 to 30 minutes. Cool in the pans on wire racks for 10 minutes. Use a knife to loosen the cake layers from the sides of the pans and invert onto the wire racks. Peel off the parchment paper and cool completely.

③ FROST THE CAKE: Slice cake layers horizontally in half. Place a split cake layer on a cake plate. Cover the top with buttercream. Repeat with the remaining 3 layers. Spread the remaining buttercream over the sides of the cake. Refrigerate the cake until 15 minutes before serving. Store refrigerated for up to 4 days.

Coffee Buttercream

2 teaspoons boiling water

2 teaspoons espresso powder

8 large egg whites

1¹/₂ cups sugar

¹/₂ teaspoon cream of tartar

¹/₈ teaspoon salt

2 cups unsalted butter (4 sticks), softened

MAKE THE BUTTERCREAM: Mix the boiling water and espresso in a small bowl and set aside. Combine the egg whites and sugar in the large bowl of an electric mixer. Set over, but not touching, a saucepan of simmering water. Whisk by hand until the sugar melts and the mixture reaches 120°F on a candy thermometer. Remove from the heat and beat with the mixer set on high speed until soft peaks form. Add the cream of tartar and salt and continue to beat until the mixture is at room temperature. Beat in the butter, 1 table-spoon at a time, until incorporated and the mixture is smooth. Beat in the espresso mixture and set aside.

NUTRITION INFORMATION PER SERVING—PROTEIN: 4.9 G; FAT: 33 G; CARBOHYDRATE: 50.3 G; FIBER: 1 G; SODIUM: 219 MG; CHOLESTEROL: 125 MG; CALORIES: 504.

Golden Ricotta Cheesecake

Shot through with golden raisins and orange zest and baked to a lovely hue,
this cheesecake glistens with orange segments and mint leaves. For the creamiest cheesecake,
use whole-milk ricotta. ✳ MAKES 12 SERVINGS (ONE 9-INCH CAKE)

1¼ cups shortbread cookie crumbs

1 cup sugar

¼ cup butter (½ stick), melted

1 cup golden raisins

24 ounces ricotta cheese

¼ cup pine nuts, toasted

1 tablespoon grated orange zest

3 large eggs

1 teaspoon vanilla extract

① MAKE THE CRUST: Preheat the oven to 350°F. Combine the cookie crumbs, ¼ cup of the sugar, and butter in a medium bowl. Press the mixture into the bottom of a 9- or 10-inch springform pan. Bake until the crust is set—about 10 minutes. Set aside.

② MAKE THE FILLING: Pour enough boiling water over the raisins to cover in a medium bowl and let stand for 5 minutes; drain. Combine the ricotta cheese, pine nuts, raisins, and zest in a large bowl. Beat the eggs in another large bowl using a mixer set on medium speed—about 2 minutes. Add the remaining sugar and vanilla and beat until thickened—about 2 minutes. Reduce the speed to low, add the ricotta mixture, and mix until combined. Pour the filling into the prepared crust and spread evenly.

③ BAKE THE CHEESECAKE: Bake until the top is golden brown and the center of the cake jiggles slightly—50 to 60 minutes. Cool in the pan on a wire rack for 2 hours. Cover and chill for several hours or overnight. Remove the rim of the pan to serve. Store refrigerated for up to 4 days.

NUTRITION INFORMATION PER SERVING—PROTEIN: 10.5 G; FAT: 14.9 G; CARBOHYDRATE: 39 G;
FIBER: .7 G; SODIUM: 142 MG; CHOLESTEROL: 83.1 MG; CALORIES: 319.

Nutmeg Sweet-Potato Cake

A great alternative to the usual holiday pie, this spicy cake is festively garnished with a candied orange rind wreath. The cake is also delicious enough to enjoy without frosting, if you like.

✻ MAKES 12 SERVINGS (ONE 9-INCH 2-LAYER CAKE)

2 cups all-purpose flour

1 1/2 teaspoons baking powder

1 teaspoon fresh grated nutmeg

1/4 teaspoon baking soda

1/4 teaspoon salt

3 large eggs

1 cup firmly packed light brown sugar

1/2 cup butter (1 stick), softened

12 ounces sweet potatoes, baked, skinned, and mashed

1/2 cup buttermilk

1/2 cup dark raisins

Orange Frosting and Candied Rind (recipe follows)

Whole nutmegs and fresh rosemary sprigs (optional)

① MAKE THE BATTER: Preheat the oven to 350°F. Grease two 9-inch cake pans. Dust with flour and tap out any excess. Set aside. Combine the flour, baking powder, nutmeg, baking soda, and salt in a medium bowl. Set aside. Separate the eggs, placing the whites in a medium bowl and the yolks in a cup. Cream the brown sugar and butter in a large bowl with a mixer set on medium speed. Add the yolks and beat until fluffy. Add the sweet potatoes and beat until smooth. Reduce the mixer speed to low and add the flour mixture by thirds, alternating with the buttermilk and ending with the dry ingredients, mixing just until the batter is smooth. Beat the egg whites in a medium bowl with clean beaters until soft peaks form. Carefully fold the beaten whites and raisins into the batter.

② BAKE THE CAKE: Divide the batter equally between the prepared pans and spread evenly. Bake until a tester inserted into the center of each cake layer comes out clean—30 to 35 minutes. Cool in the pans on wire racks 10 minutes. Use a knife to loosen the cake layers from the sides of the pans and invert the cakes onto the wire racks to cool completely.

③ ASSEMBLE THE CAKE: Line the edges of a serving plate with 3-inch-wide strips of waxed or parchment paper and place a cake layer, upside down, on top. Place one third of the Orange Frosting on top of the layer and spread evenly. Place the second layer, right side up, on top and cover the top and sides of the cake with the remaining frosting. Arrange the candied orange rind around the top edge of the cake to form a border. Surround the cake with whole nutmegs and rosemary sprigs, if desired, and serve.

NUTRITION INFORMATION PER SERVING WITHOUT NUTMEGS OR ROSEMARY—PROTEIN: 6 G; FAT: 24 G; CARBOHYDRATE: 87 G; FIBER: 2 G; SODIUM: 370 MG; CHOLESTEROL: 117 MG; CALORIES: 572.

Orange Frosting and Candied Rind

2 navel oranges

1 8-ounce package cream cheese, softened

¹/₂ cup (1 stick) butter, softened

1 1-pound package (3¹/₂ cups)
    confectioners' sugar

1 teaspoon vanilla extract

2 tablespoons granulated sugar

Grate the zest from half of 1 orange; reserve the orange. Beat the cream cheese and butter in a medium bowl with a mixer set on medium speed until blended. Reduce the mixer speed to low and beat in the confectioners' sugar, vanilla, and grated orange zest until smooth. Set aside. Use a vegetable peeler to peel the remaining zest from the reserved orange. Completely peel the remaining orange and remove the white membrane just under the rind. (Reserve the peeled oranges for another use.) Trim the edges of the rind even and cut the rind into thin strips. Discard the scraps. Combine the rind strips with enough water to cover in a 1-quart saucepan. Bring to a boil over high heat. Reduce the heat to low and cook for 2 minutes; drain well. Add the granulated sugar to the rind in the saucepan and cook over low heat until the orange strips are glazed—about 5 minutes. Set aside to cool.

Pumpkin Spice Cake

We've taken the familiar ingredients of a traditional pumpkin pie and combined them to create this spectacular dessert. One bite of this cake and the traditional pumpkin pie may have to make room on the sideboard for a new holiday favorite. ✱ MAKES 16 SERVINGS (ONE 8-INCH 3-LAYER CAKE)

1 cup pumpkin purée

1/2 cup buttermilk

1 teaspoon vanilla extract

2 cups all-purpose flour

2 teaspoons baking powder

1 1/2 teaspoons ground cinnamon

1 teaspoon baking soda

1/2 teaspoon freshly ground nutmeg

3/4 cup unsalted butter (1 1/2 sticks), softened

1 cup firmly packed dark brown sugar

1 cup granulated sugar

3 large eggs

Pumpkin Cream-Cheese Frosting (recipe follows)

① MAKE THE BATTER: Preheat the oven to 350°F. Lightly butter three 8-inch cake pans. Line the bottoms with parchment paper and butter the paper. Set aside. Combine the pumpkin purée, buttermilk, and vanilla in a medium bowl and set aside. Combine the flour, baking powder, cinnamon, baking soda, and nutmeg in a large bowl and set aside. Beat the butter in a large bowl with a mixer set on medium speed until smooth. Add the sugars and beat until smooth. Add the eggs, one at a time, beating well after each addition, until the mixture is smooth and light. Reduce the mixer speed to low and add the flour mixture by thirds, alternating with the buttermilk mixture and ending with the dry ingredients, blending until smooth after each addition.

② BAKE THE CAKE: Divide the batter equally among the prepared pans and spread evenly. Bake until a tester inserted into the center of each cake layer comes out clean—35 to 40 minutes. Cool in the pans on wire racks for 30 minutes. Use a knife to loosen the cake layers from the sides of the pans and invert the layers onto the wire racks. Peel off the parchment paper and cool completely.

③ FROST THE CAKE: Place a cake layer on a cake plate, top with a rounded cup of the Pumpkin Cream-Cheese Frosting, and spread evenly. Repeat with the remaining layers and frosting. Store refrigerated for up to 4 days.

Pumpkin Cream-Cheese Frosting

1 8-ounce package cream cheese, softened

1/4 cup canned pumpkin purée

1/4 cup unsalted butter (1/2 stick), softened

1 tablespoon fresh orange juice

1 teaspoon grated orange zest

1/2 teaspoon vanilla extract

4 cups confectioners' sugar, sifted

MAKE THE FROSTING: Beat the cream cheese, pumpkin purée, butter, orange juice, orange zest, and vanilla in a large bowl with a mixer set on medium speed until smooth. Gradually add the confectioners' sugar and beat until light and creamy—about 5 more minutes.

NUTRITION INFORMATION PER SERVING—PROTEIN: 4.6 G; FAT: 17.7 G; CARBOHYDRATE: 60.8 G; FIBER: 1.5 G; SODIUM: 195 MG; CHOLESTEROL: 86.8 MG; CALORIES: 414.

Maple Walnut Cake

A rich and buttery all-American classic with real New England flavor, this cake is superb
with the Maple-Sugar Frosting. For even more maple taste, the layers and frosting are both generously
doused with maple syrup. A garnish of candied walnuts and maple sugar suggests the flavors
within before the first piece is sliced. ✳ MAKES 12 SERVINGS (ONE 8-INCH 2-LAYER CAKE)

2 1/2 cups all-purpose flour

2 teaspoons baking powder

2 teaspoons baking soda

1/2 teaspoon salt

1/2 teaspoon ground cinnamon

1/2 cup unsalted butter (1 stick), softened

1/2 cup granulated sugar

2 large eggs

1 1/2 cups pure maple syrup

2 teaspoons vanilla extract

1/2 cup water

1 cup finely chopped walnuts

6 walnut halves

Maple-Sugar Frosting (recipe follows)

① MAKE THE BATTER: Preheat the oven to 350°F. Lightly coat two 9-inch cake pans with butter or vegetable-oil cooking spray. Dust with flour and tap out any excess. Set aside. Sift the flour, baking powder, baking soda, salt, and cinnamon together into a medium bowl. Set aside. Beat the butter and sugar in a large bowl using a mixer set on high speed for 1 minute. Add the eggs, one at a time, beating for 1 minute after each addition. Beat in 1 cup of the maple syrup and the vanilla. Reduce the mixer speed to low and add the flour mixture by thirds, alternating with the water and ending with the dry ingredients, mixing just until the batter is smooth. Gently stir in the walnuts.

② BAKE THE CAKE: Divide the batter equally between the prepared pans and spread evenly. Bake until a tester inserted into the center of each cake layer comes out clean—about 30 minutes. Cool in the cake pans on wire racks for 10 minutes. Use a knife to loosen the cake layers from the sides of the pans and invert the layers onto the wire racks to cool completely.

③ MAKE THE CAKE GARNISHES: Lightly coat a shallow baking pan with cooking spray and arrange the walnut halves about 3 to 4 inches apart. Cook the remaining 1/2 cup maple syrup over medium-high heat in a small saucepan until it reaches hard-crack stage (300°F) on a candy thermometer (a drop of the syrup placed in a glass of cold water will become hard and brittle). Remove from the heat and carefully spoon the boiled syrup over the walnuts, allowing it to run in streams around the pan. Set aside to cool completely.

④ FROST THE CAKE: Use a serrated knife to level the tops of the cake layers, if necessary. Line the edges of a cake plate with 3-inch-wide strips of waxed or parchment paper and place a cake layer, trimmed side down, on top. Place 1 cup of the Maple-Sugar Frosting on top of the layer and spread evenly. Place the second layer, trimmed side down, on the first and cover the top and sides of the cake with the remaining icing. Decorate the top of the cake with candied walnuts and the hardened maple sugar. Remove the paper strips and serve. Store at room temperature for up to 4 days.

(CONTINUED)

Maple-Sugar Frosting

2¹/₄ cups confectioners' sugar

¹/₂ cup firmly packed dark brown sugar

8 tablespoons unsalted butter (1 stick),
  softened

¹/₈ teaspoon salt

¹/₂ cup pure maple syrup

1 teaspoon vanilla extract

2 to 4 tablespoons milk

MAKE THE FROSTING: Beat the sugars, butter, and salt in a medium bowl with a mixer set on medium speed until blended. Continue beating, adding the maple syrup in a slow stream. Add the vanilla. Increase the speed to medium-high and continue to beat until light and fluffy. Add up to 4 tablespoons milk to achieve a smooth spreading consistency, if necessary.

NUTRITION INFORMATION PER SERVING—PROTEIN: 4.5 G; FAT: 18.4 G; CARBOHYDRATE: 93.3 G; FIBER: 1 G; SODIUM: 845 MG; CHOLESTEROL: 77.6 MG; CALORIES: 549.

Brown-Sugar Pound Cake

The combination of dark brown sugar, nutmeg, and vanilla gives these mini pound cakes a somewhat exotic aroma and flavor. Wrap the loaves in parchment and tie with string for nice old-fashioned hostess gifts during the holidays. * MAKES 16 SERVINGS (FOUR 5- BY 2-INCH CAKES)

3 cups cake flour
1/2 teaspoon salt
1/4 teaspoon baking soda
1/4 teaspoon ground nutmeg
1 1/2 cups unsalted butter (2 1/2 sticks), softened
1 1/2 cups firmly packed dark brown sugar
1/2 cup granulated sugar
5 large eggs
1 teaspoon vanilla extract
1/2 cup buttermilk

① MAKE THE BATTER: Preheat the oven to 350°F. Lightly coat four 5- by 2 1/2-inch mini loaf pans with vegetable-oil cooking spray and set aside. Sift the flour, salt, baking soda, and nutmeg into a medium bowl. Beat the butter and sugars in a large bowl using a mixer set on high speed until light and fluffy—about 5 minutes. Add the eggs, one at a time, beating well after each addition. Add the vanilla. Reduce the mixer speed to low and add the flour mixture by thirds, alternating with the buttermilk and ending with the dry ingredients, mixing just until the batter is smooth.

② BAKE THE CAKE: Divide the batter equally between the prepared pans and bake until a tester inserted into the center of each cake comes out clean—40 to 50 minutes. Cool in the pans on wire racks for 10 minutes. Use a knife to loosen the cakes from the sides of the pans and invert onto the wire racks to cool completely.

NUTRITION INFORMATION PER ONE-INCH SERVING—PROTEIN: 3.8 G; FAT: 16.2 G; CARBOHYDRATE: 34.1 G; FIBER: .3 G; SODIUM: 122 MG; CHOLESTEROL: 106 MG; CALORIES: 295.

Lemon Cakes with Berry Salsa

These lemon-scented mini cakes are "baked" in an unusual way: They are tightly covered and steamed on the stovetop, which makes them very moist and delectable. ✶ MAKES 5 SERVINGS

9 tablespoons butter (1 stick plus
    1 tablespoon), softened
1 1/4 cups fresh bread crumbs
3/4 cup all-purpose flour
1/2 teaspoon baking powder
1/4 teaspoon salt
2/3 cup sugar
1 large egg
5 tablespoons fresh lemon juice
1 tablespoon grated lemon zest
4 large egg whites, at room temperature
2 1/4 cups fresh berries, such as hulled
    strawberries, blueberries, and
    raspberries
2 tablespoons orange-flavored liqueur
1 tablespoon finely chopped peeled
    fresh ginger

① MAKE THE BATTER: Lightly coat five 6-ounce ramekins with 1 tablespoon butter and set aside. Half-fill a 13- by 9-inch baking pan with water, fit a wire rack in the bottom of the pan, and bring the water to a boil over high heat. Reduce the heat to low. Sift the bread crumbs, flour, baking powder, and salt together into a medium bowl and set aside. Beat the remaining butter and 1/3 cup of the sugar in a large bowl with a mixer set on high speed until light and fluffy—about 5 minutes. Add the egg and mix until just combined. Add the flour mixture, 1 tablespoon of the lemon juice, and the lemon zest and beat just until combined. Beat the egg whites in a clean large bowl with clean beaters on high speed until stiff peaks form. Gently fold the beaten egg whites into the batter until incorporated.

② STEAM THE CAKES: Divide the cake batter equally among the prepared ramekins and cover each tightly with aluminum foil. Place the ramekins in the prepared pan. Tightly cover the pan with a metal lid or foil, increase the heat to medium, and steam for 20 to 25 minutes. Remove the pan from the heat, carefully remove the lid or foil, and cover the pan with a damp clean kitchen cloth. Cool to room temperature and run a knife around the edge of the ramekins to release the cakes.

③ MAKE THE FRUIT SALSA: Combine the berries, liqueur, remaining lemon juice, 1/3 cup sugar, and ginger and lightly mash with a fork. Let the mixture stand until the berries release their juice—about 30 minutes. Spoon the salsa over the cakes and serve.

NUTRITION INFORMATION PER SERVING—PROTEIN: 8.5 G; FAT: 13.4 G; CARBOHYDRATE: 59.6 G; FIBER: 2.8 G; SODIUM: 370 MG; CHOLESTEROL: 31 MG; CALORIES: 387.

Four-Layer Gingerbread Cake

Some of the finest gifts are edible. This boxlike four-layer cake is wrapped in white-chocolate buttercream and "tied" with a chocolate ribbon for a pretty presentation. ✳ MAKES 24 SERVINGS (ONE 9-INCH 4-LAYER CAKE)

5 cups all-purpose flour

5 teaspoons ground ginger

4 teaspoons baking soda

2 teaspoons ground cinnamon

1 teaspoon ground allspice

1 teaspoon ground nutmeg

1 teaspoon salt

1/2 teaspoon ground cloves

2 cups boiling water

1 1/2 cups dark molasses

1/2 cup orange juice

1 cup unsalted butter (2 sticks), softened

1 cup firmly packed light brown sugar

4 large eggs

2 teaspoons grated orange zest

White-Chocolate Buttercream
(recipe follows)

Chocolate Ribbon (recipe follows)

① MAKE THE BATTER: Preheat the oven to 350°F. Lightly coat four 9-inch square cake pans with vegetable-oil cooking spray. Set aside. Combine the flour, ginger, baking soda, cinnamon, allspice, nutmeg, salt, and cloves in a large bowl. Set aside. Combine the boiling water, molasses, and orange juice in a 4-cup glass measuring cup or medium bowl. Set aside. Beat the butter in a large bowl with a mixer set on medium-high speed for 3 minutes. Add the brown sugar and continue to beat until light and fluffy—about 3 more minutes. Reduce the speed to low and add the eggs, one at a time, beating well after each addition. Beat in the orange zest. Add the flour mixture by thirds, alternating with the molasses mixture and ending with the dry ingredients, until the batter is smooth.

② BAKE THE CAKE: Divide the batter equally among the prepared pans and bake until a tester inserted in the center of the cake layers comes out clean— 20 to 25 minutes. Cool in the cake pans on wire racks for 5 minutes. Use a knife to loosen the cake layers from the sides of the pans and invert the layers onto the wire racks to cool completely.

③ ASSEMBLE THE CAKE: Line the edges of a cake plate with 3-inch-wide strips of waxed or parchment paper and place a cake layer on top. Place 2/3 cup White-Chocolate Buttercream on top of the layer and spread evenly. Repeat with 2 more cake layers. Place the fourth cake layer on top and spread a thin layer of buttercream over the assembled layers to seal the crumbs. Chill for 20 minutes. Use the remaining buttercream to frost the top and sides of the cake. Place the ribbon on the cake and refrigerate up to 8 hours. Set the cake out at room temperature for 30 minutes before serving.

(CONTINUED)

NUTRITION INFORMATION PER CAKE SERVING WITH BUTTERCREAM BUT WITHOUT RIBBON—PROTEIN: 6.8 G; FAT: 35.2 G; CARBOHYDRATE: 54.5 G; FIBER: 1.1 G; SODIUM: 345.8 MG; CHOLESTEROL: 214 MG; CALORIES: 594.

NUTRITION INFORMATION PER RIBBON SERVING—PROTEIN: .06 G; FAT: 1.9 G; CARBOHYDRATE: 6.8 G; FIBER: 1.9 G; SODIUM: 4.2 MG; CHOLESTEROL: 0; CALORIES: 42.

White-Chocolate Buttercream

3 cups water

12 large egg whites

$^{1}/_{2}$ cup granulated sugar

$2^{1}/_{4}$ cups unsalted butter ($4^{1}/_{2}$ sticks),
softened

18 ounces white chocolate, melted
and cooled

MAKE THE BUTTERCREAM: Bring the water to a boil in a 3-quart saucepan and reduce the heat to maintain a slow simmer. Combine the egg whites and sugar in a large bowl and set over the simmering water, making sure the bottom of the bowl does not touch the water. Whisk by hand or with a hand mixer set on low speed until the sugar dissolves and the mixture is very hot to the touch—7 to 10 minutes. Remove the bowl from heat and beat at high speed until the whites are glossy and thoroughly cooled—7 to 10 more minutes. Add the butter to the beaten whites, 2 tablespoons at a time, and beat just until incorporated. As the butter is added, the frosting may appear curdled. The frosting will become smooth and glossy as it continues to be beaten. Gradually add the white chocolate and beat until the frosting is fluffy—about 5 more minutes.

Chocolate Ribbon

3 cups water

4 ounces semisweet chocolate, chopped

3 tablespoons light corn syrup

1 tablespoon unsweetened cocoa for
sprinkling onto work surface

PREPARE THE CHOCOLATE: Bring the water to a boil in a 3-quart saucepan and reduce to a slow simmer. Place the chocolate in a medium bowl and set the bowl over the simmering water, making sure the bottom of the bowl does not touch the water. Stir the chocolate until it melts, then remove from the heat.

MAKE THE CHOCOLATE RIBBON: Stir the corn syrup into the melted chocolate until the mixture is thoroughly blended and forms a soft ball. Wrap in plastic and let stand at room temperature until the mixture reaches the consistency of modeling clay—about 30 minutes. (If preparing a day ahead, wrap tightly in plastic and store at room temperature. To use, knead the still-wrapped dough until pliable.)

FORM THE RIBBON: Remove the plastic wrap and sprinkle the work surface with the cocoa. Roll out the chocolate modeling ribbon into a narrow rectangle $^{1}/_{4}$ to $^{1}/_{8}$ inch thick. With a pastry wheel or tip of a sharp knife, cut 2 strips of ribbon, each about 13 inches long and 1 inch wide. Cut a V into each end of ribbon. Crisscross the strips of ribbon over the cake to resemble a gift package.

Pound Cake

A slice of pound cake can be the base for all sorts of toppings: Berries, ice cream,
and whipped cream all make perfect complements to this moist, buttery cake.

✳ MAKES 20 SERVINGS (TWO 9-INCH BY 5-INCH LOAF CAKES)

3 cups sifted cake flour

1/2 teaspoon salt

1/4 teaspoon baking powder

1/4 teaspoon baking soda

1 cup (2 sticks) unsalted butter, softened

2 1/2 cups sugar

3/4 teaspoon vanilla extract

1/4 teaspoon almond extract

6 large eggs, at room temperature

1 cup sour cream

① MAKE THE BATTER: Preheat the oven to 325°F. Grease a 10-inch springform pan, dust with flour, and tap out any excess. Set aside. Combine the
flour, salt, baking powder, and baking soda in a medium bowl. Beat the butter
and sugar in a large bowl with a mixer set on medium speed until light and
fluffy—about 5 minutes. Beat in the vanilla and almond extracts. Add the
eggs, one at a time, beating well after each addition. Add the flour mixture by
thirds, alternating with the sour cream and ending with the dry ingredients.
Mix just enough to blend the batter after each addition.

② BAKE THE CAKE: Pour the batter into the prepared pan and spread evenly.
Bake until a tester inserted into the center of the cake comes out clean—about
1 hour and 20 minutes. Cool in the pan on a wire rack for 10 minutes. Use a
knife to loosen the cake from the sides of the pan and release the rim of the
pan. Cool completely on the wire rack.

NUTRITION INFORMATION PER SERVING—PROTEIN: 4 G; FAT: 13.2 G; CARBOHYDRATE: 41.7 G;
FIBER: 0.4 G; SODIUM: 109 MG; CHOLESTEROL: 92.6 MG; CALORIES: 299.

Chocolate Roulade

From the French word for "to roll," this roulade is a chocolate lover's dream. Each slice of filled and rolled chocolate cake is glazed with a dark chocolate coating, then garnished with a tiny chocolate rosette. Embellish the slices with whipped cream and sprigs of mint for added flair. ✳ MAKES 28 SERVINGS

1 cup all-purpose flour

²/₃ cup unsweetened cocoa

1 teaspoon baking powder

¹/₂ teaspoon baking soda

¹/₄ teaspoon salt

8 large eggs, separated, at room temperature

1¹/₃ cups granulated sugar

2 teaspoons vanilla extract

²/₃ cup water

Confectioners' sugar

Syrup (recipe follows)

Chocolate Rosettes and Filling (recipe follows)

Chocolate Glaze (recipe follows)

① MAKE THE BATTER: Preheat the oven to 375°F. Coat two 15½- by 10½- by 1-inch jelly-roll pans with vegetable-oil cooking spray. Line the bottoms with parchment or waxed paper and lightly spray the paper. Set aside.

② Combine the flour, cocoa, baking powder, baking soda, and salt in a medium bowl. Set aside. Beat the egg whites in a large bowl with a mixer on high speed until foamy. Gradually beat in ²/₃ cup of the granulated sugar in a thin, steady stream until stiff peaks form. Set the beaten whites aside. Beat the egg yolks and vanilla in a small bowl with the mixer on high speed, until well mixed. Gradually beat in the remaining granulated sugar until thick and lemon colored. Reduce the mixer speed to low and beat in the flour mixture alternately with the water until the batter is smooth. Stir about 1 cup beaten whites into the chocolate mixture to lighten it, then gently fold the chocolate mixture into the remaining beaten whites.

③ BAKE THE CAKES: Divide the batter equally between the prepared pans and spread evenly. Bake until the center of each cake springs back when lightly touched—12 to 15 minutes. Meanwhile, sprinkle 2 clean kitchen towels with confectioners' sugar. Use a knife to loosen the cakes from the sides of the pans. Invert each cake onto a sugar-coated towel. Peel off the paper and trim ⅛ inch from around each cake to remove the crisp edges. Starting from one of the long sides, roll up each cake with the towel. Place the rolled cakes, seam side down, on wire racks to cool completely.

④ FILL THE CAKES: Gently unroll 1 cake and drizzle half the syrup over the top. Evenly spread half of the filling over the cake. Tightly roll up cake, without the towel, and wrap in plastic wrap. Repeat with the second cake. Place the cakes on a tray and refrigerate. Cakes may be assembled ahead, wrapped in plastic wrap, and refrigerated overnight or frozen, but thaw before proceeding.

⑤ GLAZE THE CAKES: With a serrated knife, using a sawing motion, cut each cake roll crosswise into 14 slices, wiping the knife clean between cuts. Reshape the slices into perfect ovals, if necessary. Stand the slices on wire racks set over waxed paper to catch any drips. Spoon about 1 tablespoon Glaze over the top of each cake slice and with a small metal spatula, quickly spread the Glaze on the top and side to seal in the crumbs. Place the racks of cakes in jelly-roll pans and refrigerate until the Glaze sets—about 15 minutes. Scrape up any drips from the waxed paper and stir into the remaining Glaze. If the Glaze hardens, microwave for 1 minute until it flows. Quickly spread more Glaze to coat the slices a second time and refrigerate until set. Cover the cakes with a third coat of Glaze to form a final smooth layer and refrigerate. Reheat the chocolate drips with the remaining Glaze for the last coating, if necessary. Top each slice with a Chocolate Rosette.

Syrup

1/4 cup granulated sugar

1/4 cup water

2 tablespoons liqueur, such as Chambord, Cointreau, or Frangelico

MAKE THE SYRUP: Combine the sugar and water in a 1-quart saucepan and bring to a boil over medium-high heat, stirring until the sugar dissolves. Remove from the heat and stir in the liqueur. Refrigerate in a covered container for up to 1 week.

Chocolate Rosettes and Filling

1 12-ounce package semisweet chocolate chips (2 cups)

1 1/2 cups heavy cream

2 tablespoons unsalted butter

2 tablespoons light corn syrup

PREPARE THE ROSETTES AND FILLING: Combine the semisweet chocolate chips, heavy cream, butter, and light corn syrup in a 2-quart saucepan. Cook over medium heat, stirring constantly, until the mixture thickens and begins to boil. Pour into a medium bowl. Place in a bowl of ice water and cool to room temperature. Or cover the surface directly with plastic wrap to prevent a skin from forming and refrigerate until cool—about 2 hours. Before assembling the cake, let the mixture stand at room temperature until slightly softened and pliable. With an electric mixer, beat just until fluffy like whipped cream. (Do not overbeat or it will curdle.) Spoon 1/3 cup of the mixture into a small pastry bag fitted with a small star tip. Set aside the remaining mixture for the Filling. Pipe out twenty-eight 1/2-inch chocolate rosettes on waxed paper and freeze until firm.

Chocolate Glaze

2 cups heavy cream

2 8-ounce packages semisweet chocolate squares or bars or 1 pound bittersweet chocolate, chopped

MAKE THE GLAZE: Heat the heavy cream to boiling in a small saucepan. Add the chocolate and let stand for 2 minutes. Gently whisk until the chocolate has melted and the mixture is smooth. Cool to room temperature.

NUTRITION INFORMATION PER SERVING—PROTEIN: 5 G; FAT: 24 G; CARBOHYDRATE: 34 G; FIBER: 2 G; SODIUM: 92 MG; CHOLESTEROL: 104 MG; CALORIES: 346.

Chocolate Cream Cakes

Cakelike on the outside and creamy on the inside, these decadent little cakes offer the perfect combination of textures in every bite. ✱ MAKES 18 SERVINGS (18 2½-INCH CAKES)

1¾ cups unsalted butter (3½ sticks), softened, plus 1 tablespoon butter, melted

2 cups plus 2½ tablespoons all-purpose flour

2¼ cups milk

⅔ cup granulated sugar

½ cup firmly packed dark brown sugar

½ cup unsweetened cocoa

3 large eggs

¼ cup sour cream

3 teaspoons vanilla extract

1 teaspoon baking powder

1 teaspoon baking soda

1 teaspoon salt

1 cup confectioners' sugar

9 ounces bittersweet chocolate, chopped

1½ tablespoons vegetable shortening

① MAKE THE BATTER: Preheat the oven to 350°F. Using a small brush, lightly coat three 2½-inch 6-cup muffin pans with the melted butter. Dust the pans with flour and tap out any excess. Combine the 2 cups flour, 1¼ cups of the milk, sugars, cocoa, ¾ cup of the butter, eggs, sour cream, 2 teaspoons vanilla, baking powder, baking soda, and salt in a large bowl. Beat using a mixer set on low speed until blended. Increase the mixer speed to medium and continue to beat until the batter is smooth—3 more minutes.

② BAKE THE CAKES: Divide the batter equally among the prepared pans and bake until the cake tops spring back when lightly touched—20 to 25 minutes. Cool in the muffin pans on a wire rack for 5 minutes. Use a knife to loosen the cakes from the sides of the pans. Invert the cakes onto the wire rack to cool completely.

③ MAKE THE CREAM FILLING: Whisk the remaining milk and flour together in a medium saucepan until smooth. Place the saucepan over medium heat and cook, stirring constantly, until thick—about 5 minutes. Remove from the heat, cool to room temperature, and set aside. Beat the remaining butter and confectioners' sugar in a medium bowl using a mixer set on high speed until light. Add the remaining vanilla, reduce the mixer speed to medium, and slowly add the cooled milk mixture. Beat for 1 more minute.

④ FILL THE CAKES: Fill a pastry bag fitted with a long narrow tip (we used a Bismark tube #230) with the cream filling. Insert the tip into the bottom of a cake and fill by gently moving the tip from side to side while squeezing the pastry bag until the cake begins to swell. Gently remove the tip and return the cake to the wire rack. Fill the remaining cakes and set the wire rack over a baking pan.

⑤ GLAZE THE CAKES: Melt the chocolate and the shortening in a double boiler set over simmering water. Remove from the heat and let sit for 3 minutes. Pour 1 tablespoon of the chocolate mixture on the top of a cake. Use a small metal spatula to spread the glaze over the top and sides of the cake until coated. Repeat with the remaining cakes. Freeze the cakes for 3 minutes, and then let sit at room temperature until the chocolate has set—about 1 hour. Decorate the cake tops with the remaining cream filling, if desired.

NUTRITION INFORMATION PER CAKE—PROTEIN: 5.5 G; FAT: 28 G; CARBOHYDRATE: 39 G; FIBER: 1.6 G; SODIUM: 242 MG; CHOLESTEROL: 92.5 MG; CALORIES: 409.

Flourless Chocolate Cake

Serve this bittersweet chocolate cake warm or at room temperature; the chocolate sauce is equally delicious over ice cream or pound cake. * MAKES 8 SERVINGS (ONE 8-INCH CAKE)

CAKE:

5 large eggs

8 1-ounce bittersweet chocolate squares
    or bars

1/2 cup (1 stick) butter

2/3 cup sugar

2/3 cup ground almonds

CHOCOLATE SAUCE:

6 1-ounce bittersweet chocolate bars
    or squares

1/2 cup heavy cream

① MAKE THE BATTER: Preheat the oven to 350°F. Butter an 8-inch spring-form pan. Separate eggs, placing whites in a medium bowl and yolks in a large bowl; bring to room temperature. In the top of a double boiler, over hot, not boiling, water, heat the chocolate and butter, stirring constantly, until melted. Set aside to cool. With a mixer set on high speed, beat the egg whites until stiff peaks form. Set the egg whites aside. Using the same beaters, beat the egg yolks and sugar until thick and pale yellow—about 5 minutes. Stir the almonds and chocolate mixture into the yolk mixture. Using a rubber spatula, fold the egg whites into the chocolate-almond mixture. Pour the batter evenly into the pan.

② BAKE THE CAKE: Bake the cake until the center springs back when gently touched with a fingertip—20 to 25 minutes. Cool on a wire rack for 10 minutes. Remove the ring from the springform pan and let the cake cool 10 minutes more on a wire rack.

③ PREPARE THE CHOCOLATE SAUCE: In the top of a double boiler set over hot, not boiling, water, heat the chocolate and heavy cream, stirring constantly, until melted and well combined. Transfer the cake to a serving plate and serve with the chocolate sauce.

NUTRITION INFORMATION PER SERVING—PROTEIN: 10 G; FAT: 43 G; CARBOHYDRATE: 47 G; FIBER: 3 G; SODIUM: 149 MG; CHOLESTEROL: 181 MG: CALORIES: 572.

Fresh Berry Shortcake

Old-fashioned shortcake is always best when fresh, local berries are in season.
Strawberries and blueberries soaked in a cinnamon and anise–spiked syrup are a refreshing twist
on this traditional summer dessert. ✴ MAKES 6 SERVINGS

SPICED BERRIES:

1½ cups water

1 cup granulated sugar

⅓ cup fresh lemon juice

2 1-inch slices fresh gingerroot

1 3-inch cinnamon stick

1 star anise, crushed

1 vanilla bean, split lengthwise

1 tablespoon cognac (optional)

1 pint fresh blueberries

1 pint fresh strawberries, hulled and halved

½ pint fresh raspberries

SHORTCAKES:

2 cups self-rising all-purpose flour

3 tablespoons granulated sugar

½ cup unsalted butter, cut into pieces

¾ cup milk

½ cup plus 1 tablespoon heavy cream

1 teaspoon confectioners' sugar

① PREPARE THE SPICED BERRIES: Combine the water, granulated sugar, lemon juice, gingerroot, cinnamon, star anise, and vanilla bean in a 2-quart saucepan and bring to a boil over high heat. Reduce the heat to medium and simmer for 25 minutes. Remove from the heat and strain the mixture through a fine sieve, discarding the spices. Stir in the cognac, if using, and set the spiced liquid aside to cool completely. Add the blueberries, strawberries, and raspberries to the spiced liquid. Set aside.

② MAKE THE SHORTCAKES: Preheat the oven to 400°F. Lightly spray a baking sheet with vegetable-oil cooking spray. Set aside. Combine the flour and granulated sugar in a medium bowl. With a pastry blender or 2 knives, cut in the butter until the mixture resembles coarse crumbs. Stir in the milk until a very soft dough forms, being careful not to overwork the dough.

③ BAKE THE SHORTCAKES: Divide the dough into 6 equal pieces and drop onto the prepared baking sheet. Lightly pat each piece into a round and brush with the 1 tablespoon heavy cream. Bake until golden brown—about 20 minutes. Transfer to a wire rack and cool completely.

④ ASSEMBLE THE SHORTCAKES: Beat the remaining ½ cup heavy cream and the confectioners' sugar in a medium bowl, with a mixer on high speed, until stiff peaks form. Cut each shortcake horizontally in half. Place each bottom half on a dessert plate. Spoon about ¾ cup berry mixture over each bottom half. Spoon a heaping tablespoon of whipped cream on top of the berry mixture. Cover with the tops of the shortcakes and drizzle some spiced syrup on each plate.

NUTRITION INFORMATION PER SERVING—PROTEIN: 7 G; FAT: 26 G; CARBOHYDRATE: 88 G;
FIBER: 5 G; SODIUM: 480 MG; CHOLESTEROL: 76 MG; CALORIES: 593.

Summer Upside-Down Cake

The true magic of traditional upside-down cake comes from the crunchy glaze that forms
in the bottom of the pan as the cake bakes. Turn the concoction on its head to serve when it is done,
and the result is a base of light, sweet cake topped with glistening brown sugar–glazed fruits.

* MAKES 8 SERVINGS (ONE 9-INCH CAKE)

3/4 cup unsalted butter (1 1/2 sticks)

1/2 cup firmly packed light brown sugar

6 fresh ripe apricots (3/4 pound), cut in half and pitted

1/4 pound fresh sweet cherries, cut in half and pitted

1 cup all-purpose flour

1 teaspoon baking powder

1/2 teaspoon salt

1 cup granulated sugar

2 large eggs

2 teaspoons vanilla extract

1/2 cup sour cream

① **MAKE THE BATTER:** Preheat the oven to 350°F. Combine 1/4 cup of the butter and the brown sugar in a 2-quart saucepan and cook, stirring, over medium-low heat until the butter melts and the mixture is smooth. Pour into an ungreased 9- by 2-inch cake pan. Tilt the pan to spread the brown sugar mixture evenly. Arrange 3 apricot halves, cut side up, in the center of the pan. Place the remaining apricot halves, cut side up, in the pan. Fill in the spaces between the apricots with the cherry halves. Set aside. Combine the flour, baking powder, and salt in a small bowl. Melt the remaining 1/2 cup butter and let cool slightly. Combine the butter, granulated sugar, eggs, and vanilla in a medium bowl and beat using a mixer set on high speed until smooth—about 2 minutes. Reduce the mixer speed to low and add the flour mixture, beating just until combined. Scrape down the sides of the bowl and beat for 15 more seconds. Add the sour cream and mix just until combined. Pour the batter over the fruit and smooth gently.

② **BAKE THE CAKE:** Bake until golden brown and a tester inserted into the center of the cake comes out clean—about 1 hour. Cool in the cake pan on a wire rack for exactly 5 minutes. Place a cake stand or serving plate on top of the cake pan and turn the cake upside down onto the cake stand. Carefully lift off the cake pan. Let cool 10 minutes. Serve warm or at room temperature.

NUTRITION INFORMATION PER SERVING—PROTEIN: 4.4 G; FAT: 22 G; CARBOHYDRATE: 58 G;
FIBER: 1.4 G; SODIUM: 351 MG; CHOLESTEROL: 105 G; CALORIES: 429.

Lemon-Blackberry Cake

Just-picked blackberries, a sure sign of long, warm summer days, crown this tender Lemon-Blackberry Cake. Filled with cassis-spiked blackberry jam and coated with Lemon Buttercream, this is a homemade treat you are sure to look forward to making each year. ✳ MAKES 16 SERVINGS (ONE 9-INCH 2-LAYER CAKE)

3 cups cake flour

1 1/2 teaspoons baking powder

1 teaspoon salt

1/2 teaspoon baking soda

2 1/2 cups sugar

1 cup butter (2 sticks), softened

5 large eggs

1 teaspoon vanilla extract

1/4 cup plus 2 tablespoons fresh lemon juice

3/4 cup buttermilk

Blackberry-Cassis Jam (recipe follows)

Lemon Buttercream Frosting (recipe follows)

① MAKE THE BATTER: Preheat the oven to 350°F. Lightly coat two 9-inch cake pans with butter or vegetable-oil cooking spray. Dust with flour and tap out any excess. Set aside. Sift the flour, baking powder, salt, and baking soda together into a medium bowl and set aside. Beat the sugar and butter in a large bowl using a mixer set on medium speed until light and fluffy—about five minutes. Add the eggs, one at a time, blending well after each addition. Scrape down the sides of the bowl and beat in the vanilla. Reduce the mixer speed to low and add the flour mixture by thirds, alternating with the lemon juice and buttermilk and ending with the dry ingredients, mixing just until the batter is smooth.

② BAKE THE CAKE: Divide the batter equally between the prepared pans and spread evenly. Bake until the tops spring back when lightly touched and a tester inserted into the center of each cake layer comes out clean—20 to 30 minutes. Cool in the cake pans on wire racks for 15 minutes. Use a knife to loosen the cake layers from the sides of the pans and invert the cake layers onto the wire racks to cool completely.

③ FROST THE CAKE: Use a serrated knife to level the tops of the cake layers, if necessary. Line the edges of a serving plate with 3-inch-wide strips of waxed or parchment paper and place a cake layer, trimmed side down, on top. Use a pastry bag or a self-sealing plastic bag with a corner cut off to pipe a 1/2-inch-thick ring of Lemon Buttercream around the edge of the layer. Spread 1 1/2 cups of the Blackberry-Cassis Jam inside the buttercream ring and top with the second cake layer trimmed side down. Place 1 cup Lemon Buttercream on top of the cake and cover the top and sides with a thin coating of icing. Chill for at least 1 hour. Cover the top and sides of the cake with the remaining icing. Remove the paper strips and serve. Store refrigerated for up to 4 days.

(CONTINUED)

NUTRITION INFORMATION PER SERVING—PROTEIN: 7.3 G; FAT: 49.7 G; CARBOHYDRATE: 102 G; FIBER: 3.2 G; SODIUM: 354 MG; CHOLESTEROL: 256 MG; CALORIES: 891.

Blackberry-Cassis Jam

5 cups fresh or frozen blackberries

1 cup plus 2 tablespoons cassis

$^1/_2$ cup sugar

2 tablespoons fresh lemon juice

1 tablespoon grated lemon zest

2 tablespoons cornstarch

MAKE THE JAM: Combine the blackberries, the 1 cup cassis, sugar, lemon juice, and lemon zest in a medium nonreactive saucepan and cook over medium-low heat until the berries begin to soften—about 10 minutes. Use a slotted spoon to transfer the berries to a medium bowl. Lightly mash them and strain the berry liquid through a sieve back into the saucepan. Set the strained berries aside. Dissolve the cornstarch in the remaining 2 tablespoons cassis and stir the mixture into the hot berry juice. Bring the liquid to a boil, reduce the heat to medium low, and cook, stirring often to avoid burning, until the liquid thickens and is reduced by half—about 2 cups. Stir the reserved blackberries into the liquid. Remove from the heat and cool completely.

Lemon Buttercream Frosting

$^1/_2$ cup egg whites (about 3 large eggs)

1 cup granulated sugar

2 cups unsalted butter (4 sticks), cut into pieces

1 tablespoon grated lemon zest

1 tablespoon fresh lemon juice

MAKE THE FROSTING: Combine the egg whites and sugar in a large bowl set over a pot filled with 1 inch of simmering water. Use a whisk to beat the mixture until it is very hot to the touch (about 160°F on an instant-read thermometer). Remove from the heat. Immediately begin whipping the mixture using a mixer set on high speed until it is cool, thick, and glossy and has tripled in volume—about 5 minutes. Reduce the mixer speed to medium and add the butter—about ¼ cup at a time and beat for 5 to 10 minutes before adding more. Add the lemon zest and lemon juice and continue to beat until smooth and fluffy.

* Buttercream Frosting *

A few tips from professional bakers: Buttercream is sensitive to temperature—it may separate slightly if the temperature in the room is very warm. Reconstituting it is easy: Set the bowl of buttercream into a larger bowl of ice water and whisk until smooth. Too cold or "lumpy" with butter pieces? Beat the frosting until it is smooth. Frost the cake with a thin layer of buttercream, then chill the cake for 20 minutes. Add the final layer of frosting to the chilled cake, smoothing the top and sides to perfection. Bakers call that intermediate step the "crumb layer" and it guarantees a picture-perfect outcome.

Apple Bundt Cake

A double dose of apples—applesauce and shredded fresh—turn simple ingredients into a moist and homey Bundt cake. Use freshly picked autumn apples to ensure the best results. Drizzle warm honey on each slice if desired. ✳ MAKES 14 SERVINGS (ONE 10-INCH BUNDT CAKE)

2 cups all-purpose flour

1 1/2 cups sugar

1 teaspoon ground cinnamon

1 teaspoon baking soda

1 teaspoon baking powder

1/4 teaspoon salt

1/2 cup butter (1 stick), melted and cooled

1/2 cup sweetened applesauce

3 large eggs

2 cups peeled and shredded sweet crisp apples, such as Jonagold or Empire (about 3 apples)

1 cup chopped pecans

① MAKE THE BATTER: Preheat the oven to 350°F. Butter a 12-cup Bundt pan. Dust with flour and tap out any excess. Set aside. Combine 1¾ cups plus 2 tablespoons of the flour, sugar, cinnamon, baking soda, baking powder, salt, butter, applesauce, and eggs in a large bowl. Beat with a wooden spoon or a mixer set on medium-low speed until a thick batter forms. Toss the apples with the remaining flour in a medium bowl. Fold the apples and pecans into the batter and mix well.

② BAKE THE CAKE: Pour the batter into the prepared pan and spread evenly. Bake until a tester inserted into the center of the cake comes out clean—about 1 hour. Cool the cake in the pan on a wire rack for 15 minutes. Use a knife to loosen the cake from the sides of the pan and invert the cake onto the wire rack to cool for 30 more minutes. Serve warm or at room temperature. Store at room temperature for up to 3 days.

NUTRITION INFORMATION PER SERVING—PROTEIN: 4 G; FAT: 14 G; CARBOHYDRATE: 42 G; FIBER: 1.5 G; SODIUM: 169 MG; CHOLESTEROL: 63.4 MG; CALORIES: 298.

Pumpkin-Date Spice Cupcakes

These miniature cakes are a variation of our Pumpkin Spice Cake (page 80); dates have been added to enrich the flavor. The cakes can be made a few days in advance and stored in the refrigerator, if you like. * MAKES 1 DOZEN CUPCAKES

1²/₃ cups all-purpose flour

1 teaspoon baking soda

1 teaspoon cinnamon

³/₄ teaspoon salt

¹/₄ teaspoon baking powder

¹/₈ teaspoon ground cloves

1¹/₄ cups granulated sugar

¹/₃ cup vegetable shortening

2 large eggs

³/₄ cup canned pumpkin purée

¹/₃ cup water

¹/₃ cup chopped pitted dates

¹/₂ cup sliced almonds

Maple Cream-Cheese Frosting
   (recipe follows)

① MAKE THE BATTER: Preheat the oven to 350°F. Line 12 muffin-pan cups with paper liners and set aside. Combine the flour, baking soda, cinnamon, salt, baking powder, and cloves in a medium bowl and set aside. Beat the sugar and shortening in a large bowl using a handheld mixer on medium speed until light and fluffy—about 5 minutes. Add the eggs, one at a time, beating well after each addition. Reduce the mixer speed to low and beat in the pumpkin puree and water until blended. Using a rubber spatula, fold in the flour mixture by thirds until the batter is smooth. Stir in the dates.

② BAKE THE CUPCAKES: Fill each lined muffin cup three quarters full with batter. Bake until a tester inserted into the center of a cupcake comes out clean—25 to 30 minutes. Transfer the cupcakes to a wire rack to cool completely.

③ FROST THE CUPCAKES: Spread the Maple Cream-Cheese Frosting over the tops of the cupcakes and top with the sliced almonds.

Maple Cream-Cheese Frosting

2 ounces cream cheese, softened

2 tablespoons butter, softened

2 teaspoons fresh lemon juice

1 cup confectioners' sugar

2 tablespoons pure maple syrup

MAKE THE FROSTING: Beat the cream cheese and butter in a medium bowl with a mixer set on medium speed until blended. Add the lemon juice and confectioners' sugar, reduce the mixer speed to low, and beat until smooth. Beat in the maple syrup.

NUTRITION INFORMATION PER SERVING—PROTEIN: 4 G; FAT: 12 G; CARBOHYDRATE: 50 G; FIBER: 1.9 G; SODIUM: 273 MG; CHOLESTEROL: 46 MG; CALORIES: 323.

Coconut Hummingbird Cake

This classic Southern layer cake is flavored with pineapples, bananas, and pecans. Food writers Martha Pearl Villas and her son John Villas say the cake "might have been so named because it is so sweet, and hummingbirds are known for their love of sugar water." The easy batter is prepared in a single bowl with just a wooden spoon for the mixing. ✳ MAKES 16 SERVINGS (ONE 9-INCH 3-LAYER CAKE)

3 cups all-purpose flour

2 cups granulated sugar

1 teaspoon baking soda

1 teaspoon ground cinnamon

1/2 teaspoon salt

3 large eggs, beaten

3/4 cup vegetable oil

1 3/4 cups mashed ripe bananas
(about 2 bananas)

1 8-ounce can crushed pineapple,
undrained

1 cup chopped pecans

2 teaspoons vanilla extract

Cream Cheese Frosting (recipe follows)

1 1/2 cups unsweetened coconut flakes

① MAKE THE BATTER: Preheat the oven to 350°F. Butter three 9-inch cake pans. Dust with flour and tap out any excess. Set aside. Combine the flour, sugar, baking soda, cinnamon, and salt in a large bowl. Add the eggs and vegetable oil, stirring with a wooden spoon until the dry ingredients are moistened. Do not beat. Stir in the banana, pineapple with juice, pecans, and vanilla.

② BAKE THE CAKE: Divide the batter equally among the prepared pans. Bake until a tester inserted into the center of each cake layer comes out clean—25 to 30 minutes. Cool in the pans on wire racks for 10 minutes. Use a knife to loosen the cake layers from the sides of the pans and invert the layers onto the wire racks to cool completely.

③ FROST THE CAKE: Line the edges of a cake plate with 3-inch-wide strips of waxed or parchment paper and place a cake layer on top. Cover top with Cream Cheese Frosting and spread evenly; repeat with the second layer. Top with the third layer and cover the top and sides of the cake with the remaining frosting and sprinkle the coconut on top. Remove the paper strips and serve. Store refrigerated for up to 4 days.

Cream Cheese Frosting

1 8-ounce package cream cheese, softened

1/2 cup butter (1 stick), softened

1 teaspoon vanilla extract

1 1-pound box confectioners' sugar, sifted

MAKE THE FROSTING: Beat the cream cheese, butter, and vanilla until smooth in a medium bowl with a mixer set on medium speed until smooth. Reduce the speed to low and slowly add the confectioners' sugar, beating until the frosting has thickened and is smooth.

NUTRITION INFORMATION PER SERVING—PROTEIN: 8 G; FAT: 39 G; CARBOHYDRATE: 112 G; FIBER: 4 G; SODIUM: 321 MG; CHOLESTEROL: 93 MG; CALORIES: 812.

Strawberry Savarin

Savarin, named after the French politician and gastronome Anthelme Brillat-Savarin, is a buttery, yeast-leavened cake that is often baked in a ring mold or Bundt pan. It is a variation on the rum-soaked, raisin-stuffed dessert known as baba au rum that was created by a French pastry chef in the mid-nineteenth century. A Savarin can be served dressed with dollops of whipped cream and decorated with fresh fruit, dusted with confectioners' sugar, or sauced with strawberry-rhubarb sauce, as we've done here.

* MAKES 10 SERVINGS (ONE 10-INCH RING CAKE)

$^{1}/_{2}$ cup warm water

1 package active dry yeast

1 teaspoon plus 2 tablespoons granulated sugar

3 cups all-purpose flour

$^{1}/_{2}$ teaspoon salt

4 large eggs, beaten

$^{1}/_{2}$ cup butter (1 stick), softened

1 quart large fresh strawberries

Confectioners' sugar (optional)

Strawberry-Rhubarb Syrup (recipe follows)

① MAKE THE DOUGH: Lightly coat a 10-inch ring mold with vegetable-oil cooking spray. Set aside. Combine the water, yeast, and the 1 teaspoon granulated sugar in a small bowl, stirring to dissolve the yeast. Let stand until foamy—about 5 minutes. Combine the flour, remaining 2 tablespoons granulated sugar, and salt in a large bowl. Add the yeast mixture and eggs. With a wooden spoon, beat the flour mixture for 5 minutes (the dough will be wet). Cover the bowl with a clean kitchen towel and let the dough rise in a warm place, away from drafts, until doubled in size—about 1½ hours. With a wooden spoon, beat the butter into the dough and spoon into the prepared ring mold. Cover with the towel and let rise in a warm place until nearly doubled in size—about 1 hour.

② BAKE THE CAKE: Meanwhile, preheat the oven to 375°F. Bake until golden brown and firm—20 to 25 minutes. Let cool in the pan on a wire rack for 10 minutes. Use a knife to loosen the savarin from the sides of the pan and unmold onto the wire rack and let cool for 15 minutes.

③ ASSEMBLE THE SAVARIN: Place the savarin on a cake plate. Fill the center with strawberries and dust with confectioners' sugar, if desired. Serve with the Strawberry-Rhubarb Syrup.

Strawberry-Rhubarb Syrup

$^{3}/_{4}$ cup trimmed and chopped rhubarb

$^{1}/_{2}$ cup sliced fresh strawberries

$^{2}/_{3}$ cup granulated sugar

$^{1}/_{2}$ cup water

MAKE THE SYRUP: Combine the rhubarb, strawberries, sugar, and water in a 1-quart saucepan. Bring to a boil over medium-high heat and cook until the rhubarb is very soft—about 15 minutes. Strain the mixture through a sieve into a serving dish, discarding the rhubarb-strawberry pulp. Store refrigerated in an airtight container for up to 4 days.

NUTRITION INFORMATION PER SERVING WITHOUT CONFECTIONERS' SUGAR OR SYRUP—PROTEIN: 7 G; FAT: 12 G; CARBOHYDRATE: 49 G; FIBER: 3 G; SODIUM: 214 MG; CHOLESTEROL: 108 MG; CALORIES: 329.

NUTRITION INFORMATION PER 2-TABLESPOON SERVING OF SYRUP—PROTEIN: .1 G; FAT: .04 G; CARBOHYDRATE: 14 G; FIBER: .4 G; SODIUM: .8 MG; CHOLESTEROL: 0: CALORIES: 55.

Frozen Raspberry Layer Cake

Your guests will think you went to great lengths to put this cake together. The secret is store-bought ingredients: pound cake, ice cream, sorbet, and fresh raspberries. There's no baking, just simple assembly. Decorate the top with whipped cream, if you like. ✳ MAKES 12 SERVINGS (ONE 9-INCH 3-LAYER CAKE)

2 10³/₄-ounce frozen pound cakes, crusts removed, cut into ¼-inch-thick slices

3 cups vanilla ice cream, slightly softened

4 cups raspberry sorbet, slightly softened

1 pint fresh raspberries, rinsed

3 tablespoons Chambord or other raspberry-flavored liqueur

① PREPARE THE PAN: Trace and cut out a 9-inch circle from parchment paper and fit it into the bottom of a 9-inch springform pan. Cut out a 3- by 27-inch strip of parchment and fit around the inside of the pan. Tape to secure the parchment paper and set aside.

② ASSEMBLE THE CAKE: Cover the bottom of the pan with a single layer of pound cake slices, cutting them to fit as needed. Spread the ice cream evenly over the cake. Freeze until the ice cream hardens—about 25 minutes. Spread 2 cups of the sorbet over the ice cream and top with a second layer of pound cake slices. Return the cake to the freezer for 10 minutes. Combine the raspberries and the Chambord in a small bowl. Remove the cake pan from the freezer and spoon the berries evenly over the cake. Top with a final layer of pound cake and the remaining sorbet. Wrap tightly with plastic wrap and freeze until firm—at least 4 hours. Remove the rim of the pan. Place a flat plate on top of the cake, invert, and remove the pan bottom. Peel off the paper and invert the cake, right side up, onto a cake plate. Serve immediately.

NUTRITION INFORMATION PER SERVING—PROTEIN: 3.8 G; FAT: 10.1 G; CARBOHYDRATE: 49 G; FIBER: 1.3 G; SODIUM: 174 MG; CHOLESTEROL: 68.5 MG; CALORIES: 305.

Cinnamon Pear Torte

Made in the classic style of an old-fashioned refrigerator cake, this spiced torte is best assembled the day before serving so the layers have a chance to absorb the juicy fruit.

✱ MAKES 12 SERVINGS (ONE 6-LAYER RECTANGULAR CAKE)

2¹/₂ cups all-purpose flour

2 tablespoons ground cinnamon, plus
    additional for dusting (optional)

2 teaspoons baking powder

¹/₂ teaspoon salt

1 cup butter (2 sticks), softened

1 1-pound package light brown sugar

3 large eggs

3 teaspoons vanilla extract

2 29-ounce cans pear halves in heavy syrup,
    undrained

1 cup heavy cream

2 tablespoons confectioners' sugar

① MAKE THE CAKE: Preheat the oven to 350°F. Lightly grease two 15½- by 10½- by 1-inch jelly-roll pans. Cut two 17½- by 10½-inch sheets of waxed or parchment paper and fit into the pans, allowing the paper to extend up the short sides of the pans. Generously butter the paper. Dust with flour and tap out any excess. Set aside. Combine the flour, cinnamon, baking powder, and salt in a small bowl and set aside. Beat the butter and brown sugar in a large bowl with a mixer set on high speed until light and fluffy—about 5 minutes. Add the eggs, one at a time, beating well after each addition. Reduce the mixer speed to low and mix in 2 teaspoons of the vanilla and the flour mixture just until a thick batter forms. Divide the batter equally between the prepared pans and spread evenly to make thin layers.

② BAKE THE CAKE: Bake until the centers of the cakes appear firm—15 to 18 minutes. Use a knife to loosen the cakes from the sides of the pans and invert the cake layers onto wire racks. Remove the pans and peel off the waxed paper. Cut each layer crosswise into 3 equal pieces and set aside to cool slightly. Meanwhile, thinly slice the pears.

③ ASSEMBLE THE TORTE: Place 1 cake layer, right side up, on a serving plate. Top with one fifth of the pear slices. Repeat four times, then top with the remaining cake layer, top side down. Set aside.

④ PREPARE THE WHIPPED-CREAM FROSTING: Beat the heavy cream, confectioners' sugar, and remaining vanilla in a chilled medium bowl with a mixer set on high speed, just until stiff peaks form. Spread the cream evenly over the top and sides of the torte. Refrigerate, loosely covered, for 8 hours or up to overnight. Before serving, sprinkle a crosshatch of cinnamon over the top of the torte, if desired. Cut torte lengthwise in half and crosswise in sixths to make 12 pieces.

NUTRITION INFORMATION PER SERVING—PROTEIN: 5 G; FAT: 25 G; CARBOHYDRATE: 85 G; FIBER: .3 G; SODIUM: 336 MG; CHOLESTEROL: 122 MG; CALORIES: 567.

Chocolate Espresso Torte

This extremely rich and dark single-layer cake, a quintessentially Viennese confection, is a classic combination of chocolate and espresso. Garnish it with seasonal fruit, whipped cream, or chocolate leaves.

✱ MAKES 12 SERVINGS (ONE 9- BY 9-INCH CAKE)

21 ounces semisweet chocolate, chopped

1 1/2 cups unsalted butter (3 sticks), softened

2 tablespoons espresso powder or instant-coffee crystals

5 large eggs, separated, at room temperature

3/4 cup sugar

1/2 cup all-purpose flour

1/4 teaspoon salt

1 tablespoon vanilla extract

1/2 teaspoon cream of tartar

2 tablespoons heavy cream

1 tablespoon light corn syrup

① MAKE THE CAKE BATTER: Preheat the oven to 350°F. Butter a 9-inch square pan. Line the bottom with parchment paper and butter the paper. Set aside. Melt 9 ounces of the chocolate, 3/4 cup of the butter, and the espresso powder in a double boiler set over low heat. Remove from the heat. Beat the egg yolks in a large bowl using a mixer set on medium speed, until foamy—15 to 30 seconds. Add 1/2 cup sugar and continue to beat until thick and pale—about 3 minutes. Reduce the mixer speed to low and add the chocolate mixture, flour, salt, and vanilla. Combine the egg whites and cream of tartar in a medium bowl. Beat on medium speed until soft peaks form. Add the remaining sugar in a thin, steady stream and beat until stiff peaks form. Fold the beaten whites into the chocolate mixture by thirds until incorporated.

② BAKE THE CAKE: Pour the batter into the prepared pan and bake until a tester inserted into the center of the cake comes out clean—about 35 minutes. Cool in the pan on a wire rack for 30 minutes. Invert the cake onto a wire rack set over a baking sheet. Peel off the parchment paper.

③ MAKE THE GANACHE GLAZE: Melt the remaining 12 ounces of chocolate in a double boiler set over low heat. Remove from the heat and stir in the remaining softened butter until combined. Stir in the heavy cream and corn syrup. Allow the mixture to cool until the glaze is thick enough to coat yet still pours easily—2 to 3 minutes. Pour the glaze onto the center of the cake and use a narrow metal spatula to smooth it evenly over the top and sides. Let the cake sit until the glaze sets—about 10 minutes. Using one or two wide spatulas as an aid, carefully transfer the cake to a serving plate.

NUTRITION INFORMATION PER SERVING—PROTEIN: 3 G; FAT: 40.4 G; CARBOHYDRATE: 46.4 G; FIBER: .1 G; SODIUM: 32.8 MG; CHOLESTEROL: 154 MG; CALORIES: 548.

Stacked Applesauce Cake

Three tall layers of our easy-to-make variation of a traditional Kentucky Apple Stack Cake float on pillows of spiced whipped cream. For a clean apple flavor use white sugar, or use light brown sugar for a more classic spice-cake flavor. ✷ MAKES 16 SERVINGS (ONE 9-INCH 3-LAYER CAKE)

3 cups all-purpose flour

1 tablespoon baking soda

1 1/2 teaspoons baking powder

3/4 teaspoon ground cinnamon

3/4 teaspoon ground nutmeg

1/4 teaspoon ground cloves

3/4 cup unsalted butter (1 1/2 sticks), softened

1 1/2 cups granulated sugar

2 large eggs

1 tablespoon vanilla extract

3 cups unsweetened applesauce

Cinnamon Whipped Cream (recipe follows)

2 tablespoons confectioners' sugar (optional)

① MAKE THE BATTER: Preheat the oven to 350°F. Lightly coat three 9-inch cake pans with butter or vegetable-oil cooking spray. Dust with flour and tap out any excess. Set aside. Combine the flour, baking soda, baking powder, cinnamon, nutmeg, and cloves in a medium bowl. Set aside. Beat the butter in a large bowl using a mixer set on high speed for 1 minute. Add the granulated sugar and continue to beat until blended. Add the eggs and vanilla and beat for 2 more minutes. Reduce the mixer speed to low and add the flour mixture by thirds, alternating with the applesauce and ending with the dry ingredients, mixing just until the batter is smooth.

② BAKE THE CAKE: Divide the batter equally among the prepared pans and spread evenly. Bake until a tester inserted into the center of each cake layer comes out clean—35 to 40 minutes. Cool in the pans on wire racks for 10 minutes. Use a knife to loosen the cake layers from the sides of the pans and invert the layers onto the wire racks to cool completely.

③ ASSEMBLE THE CAKE: Place a cake layer on a cake plate or stand. Spread half the Cinnamon Whipped Cream over the layer. Place a second layer on top of the first and spread with the remaining whipped cream. Top with the last layer, sprinkle with confectioners' sugar, if desired, and serve. Store refrigerated for up to 4 days.

Cinnamon Whipped Cream

2 cups cold heavy cream

3/4 cup confectioners' sugar

1 teaspoon ground cinnamon

1/2 teaspoon vanilla extract

Make the whipped cream: Beat the heavy cream, sugar, cinnamon, and vanilla in a large bowl using a mixer set on medium-high speed until stiff peaks form. Do not overbeat.

NUTRITION INFORMATION PER SERVING—PROTEIN: 3.7 G; FAT: 20 G; CARBOHYDRATE: 48.7 G; FIBER: 1.5 G; SODIUM: 303 MG; CHOLESTEROL: 64 MG; CALORIES: 384.

Grandma Stonesifer's Spice Cake

Former *Country Living* Senior Editor Marjorie Gage has graciously shared her recipe for this easy-to-make layer cake, which was adapted from a family favorite and passed down by her husband's great-grandmother, Mary Stonesifer, of York County, Pennsylvania. Buttermilk is the secret ingredient that makes the layers so moist and tender. ✶ MAKES 16 SERVINGS (ONE 9-INCH 2-LAYER CAKE)

Vegetable-oil cooking spray
2 cups all-purpose flour
1 tablespoon Dutch-processed cocoa
2 teaspoons baking powder
1 1/2 teaspoons ground cinnamon
1 teaspoon baking soda
1/2 teaspoon ground nutmeg
1/2 teaspoon ground allspice
1/4 teaspoon ground cloves
1/2 cup unsalted butter (1 stick), softened
1/2 cup vegetable shortening
1 cup firmly packed dark brown sugar
1 cup granulated sugar
4 large eggs
1 1/4 cups buttermilk
1 teaspoon vanilla extract
Orange Cream-Cheese Frosting (recipe
  follows)

① MAKE THE BATTER: Preheat the oven to 350°F. Lightly coat two 9-inch cake pans with vegetable-oil cooking spray. Line the bottoms with parchment paper and lightly coat the paper with cooking spray. Set aside. Sift the flour, cocoa, baking powder, cinnamon, baking soda, nutmeg, allspice, and cloves together into another large bowl. Set aside. Beat the butter and shortening in a large bowl using a mixer set on medium speed until smooth. Add the sugars and beat until well blended. Add the eggs, one at a time, beating well after each addition, until the mixture is smooth and light. Set aside. Combine the buttermilk and vanilla extract in a 2-cup glass measuring cup. Reduce the mixer speed to low and add the flour mixture by thirds, alternating with the buttermilk and ending with the dry ingredients, blending the batter well after each addition.

② BAKE THE CAKE: Divide the batter equally between the prepared pans and spread evenly. Bake until a tester inserted into the center of each cake layer comes out clean—30 to 40 minutes. Cool in the cake pans on wire racks for 10 minutes. Use a knife to loosen the cake layers from the sides of the pans and invert the cake layers onto the wire racks. Peel off the parchment paper and cool completely.

③ FROST THE CAKE: Line the edges of a serving plate with 3-inch-wide strips of waxed or parchment paper and place a cake layer on top. Using an icing spatula or a table knife, spread the top of the first layer with frosting. Place the other cake layer on top of the first layer and frost the entire cake. Remove the paper strips and serve. Store refrigerated for up to 4 days.

(CONTINUED)

NUTRITION INFORMATION PER SERVING: PROTEIN: 6.43 G; FAT: 23.3 G; CARBOHYDRATE: 57.7 G; FIBER: .8 G; SODIUM: 265 MG; CHOLESTEROL: 125 MG; CALORIES: 460.

Orange Cream-Cheese Frosting

2 8-ounce packages cream cheese,
  softened

1/2 cup unsalted butter (1 stick), softened

2 tablespoons grated orange zest (about
  1 large orange)

2 tablespoons fresh orange juice

2 teaspoons vanilla extract

4 cups confectioners' sugar, sifted

MAKE THE FROSTING: Beat the cream cheese, butter, orange zest, orange juice and vanilla in a large bowl using a mixer set on medium speed until smooth. Gradually add the confectioners' sugar and beat until smooth and creamy—3 to 5 more minutes.

* Got Buttermilk? *

* True buttermilk is exactly that: the liquid skimmed off cream being churned into butter. Today, however, most dairies make buttermilk by adding live cultures to skim milk.

* If stored in a tightly covered container at 40°F, buttermilk will keep for about 2 weeks.

* Don't freeze buttermilk—it will separate.

Measurement Conversion Chart

The recipes that appear in this cookbook use the standard United States method for measuring liquid and dry or solid ingredients (teaspoons, tablespoons, and cups). The information on this chart is provided to help cooks outside the U.S. successfully use these recipes. All equivalents are approximate.

✳ METRIC EQUIVALENTS FOR DIFFERENT TYPES OF INGREDIENTS

A standard cup measure of a dry or solid ingredient will vary in weight depending on the type of ingredient. A standard cup of liquid is the same volume for any type of liquid. Use the following chart when converting standard cup measures to grams (weight) or milliliters (volume).

Standard Cup	Fine Powder (e.g. flour)	Grain (e.g. rice)	Granular (e.g. sugar)	Liquid Solids (e.g. butter)	Liquid (e.g. milk)
1	140 g	150 g	190 g	200 g	240 ml
¾	105 g	113 g	143 g	150 g	180 ml
⅔	93 g	100 g	125 g	133 g	160 ml
½	70 g	75 g	95 g	100 g	120 ml
⅓	47 g	50 g	63 g	67 g	80 ml
¼	35 g	38 g	48 g	50 g	60 ml
⅛	18 g	19 g	24 g	25 g	30 ml

✳ USEFUL EQUIVALENTS FOR LIQUID INGREDIENTS BY VOLUME

¼ tsp	=				1 ml
½ tsp	=				2 ml
1 tsp	=				5 ml
3 tsp	=	1 tbls	=	½ fl oz	15 ml
	2 tbls	=	⅛ cup	= 1 fl oz	30 ml
	4 tbls	=	¼ cup	= 2 fl oz	60 ml
	5 ⅓ tbls	=	⅓ cup	= 3 fl oz	80 ml
	8 tbls	=	½ cup	= 4 fl oz	120 ml
	10 ⅔ tbls	=	⅔ cup	= 5 fl oz	160 ml
	12 tbls	=	¾ cup	= 6 fl oz	180 ml
	16 tbls	=	1 cup	= 8 fl oz	240 ml
	1 pt	=	2 cups	= 16 fl oz	480 ml
	1 qt	=	4 cups	= 32 fl oz	960 ml
				33 fl oz	= 1000 ml = 1 l

✳ USEFUL EQUIVALENTS FOR DRY INGREDIENTS BY WEIGHT

(To convert ounces to grams, multiply the number of ounces by 30.)

1 oz	=	¹/₁₆ lb	=	30 g
4 oz	=	¼ lb	=	120 g
8 oz	=	½ lb	=	240 g
12 oz	=	¾ lb	=	360 g
16 oz	=	1 lb	=	480 g

✳ USEFUL EQUIVALENTS FOR LENGTH

(To convert inches to centimeters, multiply the number of inches by 2.5.)

1 in	=			2.5 cm
6 in	=	½ ft	=	15 cm
12 in	=	1 ft	=	30 cm
36 in	=	3 ft	= 1 yd =	90 cm
40 in	=			100 cm = 1 m

✳ USEFUL EQUIVALENTS FOR COOKING/OVEN TEMPERATURES

	Fahrenheit	Celsius	Gas Mark
Freeze Water	32° F	0° C	
Room Temperature	68° F	20° C	
Boil Water	212° F	100° C	
Bake	325° F	160° C	3
	350° F	180° C	4
	375° F	190° C	5
	400° F	200° C	6
	425° F	220° C	7
	450° F	230° C	8
Broil			Grill

Page 2: Ann Stratton; Page 6: Ann Stratton; Page 8: Beatriz Da Costa; Page 10: Dale Wing; Page 12: Ann Stratton; Page 15: Ann Stratton; Page 16: Ann Stratton; Page 20: Ericka McConnell; Page 23: Ann Stratton; Page 24: Charles Schiller; Page 27: Evan Sklar; Page 28: Ericka McConnell; Page 31: Alison Miksch; Page 32: Alan Richardson; Page 35: Ann Stratton; Page 37: Charles Schiller; Page 39: Ann Stratton; Page 40: Helen Norman; Page 44: Lisa Hubbard; Page 47: Dale Wing; Page 48: Alan Richardson; Page 51: Ryan Benyi; Page 52: Ann Stratton; Page 57: Charles Schiller; Page 58: Jonelle Weaver; Page 61: Charles Schiller; Page 63: Ann Stratton; Page 64: Ryan Benyi; Page 66: Charles Schiller; Page 68: Ann Stratton; Page 72: Alan Richardson; Page 75: Alan Richardson; Page 76: Lisa Hubbard; Page 81: Charles Schiller; Page 82: Ann Stratton; Page 87: Ann Stratton; Page 88: Keith Scott Morton; Page 95: Beatriz Da Costa; Page 96: Dennis Gottlieb; Page 99: Keith Scott Morton; Page 101: Keith Scott Morton; Page 102: Ann Stratton; Page 107: Mark Ferri; Page 108: Charles Gold; Page 111: Alan Richardson; Page 113: Charles Maraia; Page 114: Louis Wallach; Page 117: Lisa Hubbard; Page 118: Ann Stratton; Page 120: Ann Stratton; Page 124: Andrew McCaul; Page 126: Steven Randazzo

A

Angel food cake, 28, 29
Apple Bundt Cake, 105
Applesauce cakes, 26–27, 118, 119

B

Baking powder/soda, 14
Baking tips, 18–19
Banana cakes, 50–54
Berry-Dotted Angel Food Cake, 28, 29
Blackberry-Cassis Jam, 104
Blueberry Hill Cheesecake, 32, 33

C

Carrot Pistachio Cake and Cupcakes, 24, 25
Cheesecake
    Blueberry Hill, 32, 33
    Chocolate Peanut, 38–39
    Golden Ricotta, 76, 77
Cheeses, 14–17
Chocolate Cake
    Big-Top Carnival Cake, 40, 41–42
    Café au Lait, 74–75
    Chocolate Cream Cakes, 94–95
    Chocolate Espresso Torte, 116–117
    Chocolate Peanut Cheesecake, 38–39
    Chocolate Roulade, 92–93
    Easy Chocolate Party Cake, 34–35
    Flourless, 96, 97
    German, 22–23
    "Hot," 36–37
    Red Velvet Cake, 62–63

Rich Chocolate Layer Cake, 66, 67
Cinnamon Pear Torte, 115
Coconut Cloud Cake, 68, 69–70
Coconut Coffee Cake, Toasted, 60–61
Coconut Hummingbird Cake, 108, 109
Coffee Cake, 60–61
Cranberry-Apple Upside-Down Cake, 71

D

Dairy products, 14–17

E

Equipment, 17–18

F

Fig Cake, Fresh, 43
Flours, 13
Frosting
    Black Raspberry Buttercream, 65
    Caramel Icing, 54
    Chocolate Glaze/Rosettes, 93
    Chocolate Ribbon, 90
    Coffee Buttercream, 74
    Cooked Vanilla Icing, 62
    Cream-Cheese, 50, 109
    Fluffy Meringue, 70
    Lemon Buttercream, 104
    Maple-Sugar, 84
    Orange, 79
    Orange Cream-Cheese, 122
    Pumpkin Cream-Cheese, 80
    White-Chocolate Buttercream, 90

White-Chocolate Cream-Cheese, 42
Fruit Salsa, 86–87

G

Gingerbread cakes, 44, 45, 88, 89–90

I

Ingredients, 13–17

K

Kitchen's Chambord Layer Cake, 64, 65
Kitchen's Hummingbird Cake, 50–51

L

Lemon-Blackberry Cake, 102, 103–104
Lemon Cakes with Berry Salsa, 86–87
Lemon Curd, 70

M

Maple Walnut Cake, 82, 83–84
Measurement conversions, 123

N

Nutmeg Sweet-Potato Cake, 78–79

P

Pear cakes
    Cinnamon Pear Torte, 114, 115
    Pear Upside-Down Cake, 30–31
    Skillet Cake with Carmelized Pears, 55
Peppermint Cake, 46–47

Pistachio Semolina Honey Cake, 72, 73
Pound Cake, 91
    Brown Sugar, 85
    Burnt-Sugar, 58, 59
    Spice, 48, 49
Pumpkin-Date Spice Cupcakes, 106–107
Pumpkin Spice Cake, 80–81

R

Raspberry Layer Cake, Frozen, 112–113

S

Shortcake, 98–99
Skillet Cake with Carmelized Pears, 55
Spice Cake
    Grandma Stonsifer's, 120, 121–122
    Pound Cake, 48, 49
    Pumpkin, 80–81
    Pumpkin-Date Spice Cupcakes, 106–107
Strawberry Cake, Fresh, 56–57
Strawberry Savarin, 110–111
Sweeteners, 14
Sweet-Potato Cake, 78–79

U

Upside-Down Cake
    Cranberry-Apple, 71
    Pear, 30–31
    Summer, 100–101

W

Whipped cream, cinnamon, 119

The Library of Congress has cataloged the hardcover edition as follows:

Great cakes: home-baked creations from the Country living kitchen / from the editors of Country living.
     p. cm.
Includes index.
ISBN 1-58816-404-7
1. Cake. I. Country living.
TX771.G69 2005
641.8'653-dc22

2004030047

10 9 8 7 6 5 4 3 2 1

Supplemental text by Kathleen Hackett
Design by Gretchen Scoble Design

First Paperback Edition 2008
Published by Hearst Books
A Division of Sterling Publishing Co., Inc.
387 Park Avenue South, New York, NY 10016

Country Living and Hearst Books are trademarks of Hearst Communications, Inc.

www.countryliving.com

For information about custom editions, special sales, premium and corporate purchases, please contact Sterling Special Sales Department at 800-805-5489 or specialsales@sterlingpublishing.com.

Distributed in Canada by Sterling Publishing
C/o Canadian Manda Group, 165 Dufferin Street
Toronto, Ontario, Canada M6K 3H6

Distributed in Australia by Capricorn Link (Australia) Pty. Ltd.
P.O. Box 704, Windsor, NSW 2756 Australia

Manufactured in China

Sterling ISBN 13: 978-1-58816-686-9
    ISBN 10: 1-58816-686-4